Copyright Notice & Disclaimer

© **Copyright 2020 Sandeep Ravidutt Sharma - All rights reserved.**
In no way is it legal to reproduce, duplicate, or transmit any part of this document in either electronic means or in printed format. Recording of this publication is strictly prohibited and any storage of this document is not allowed unless with written permission from the publisher. All rights reserved. The information provided herein is stated to be truthful and consistent, in that any liability, in terms of inattention or otherwise, by any usage or abuse of any policies, processes, or directions contained within is the solitary and utter responsibility of the recipient reader. Under no circumstances will any legal responsibility or blame be held against the author / publisher for any reparation, damages, or monetary loss due to the information herein, either directly or indirectly. The author own all copyrights.

Legal Notice:
This book is copyright protected. This is only for personal use. You cannot amend, distribute, sell, use, quote or paraphrase any part or the content within this book without the consent of the author or copyright owner. Legal action will be pursued if this is breached.

Disclaimer Notice:
Please note the information about projects, tenders, and contracts contained in ProjectX India is collected through extensive research and is provided only for the reference of the readers. The contact information provided in this book should not be construed as an invitation by the respective company or official to solicit further business. These contacts are purely compiled from sources as available in the public domain from the respective company or official. Every attempt has been made to provide the reader accurate, up to date and reliable complete information. No warranties of any kind are expressed or implied. Readers acknowledge that the author is not engaging in the rendering of legal, financial, medical or professional advice. By reading this document, the reader agrees that under no circumstances the author / publisher is responsible for any losses, direct or indirect, which are incurred as a result of the use of information contained within this document, including, but not limited to, — errors, omissions, or inaccuracies.

If you have further questions, contact on **Tel: +918779373203**
Email: sandeepraviduttsharma@gmail.com

Dedication

This book is dedicated to **Sita Ram**. Ram or Rama is one of the most important incarnation of **Lord Vishnu** while Sita or Siya is the incarnation of **Goddess Lakshmi**. Ram denotes our Soul, or the super consciousness, truth and virtue. Sita represents the ideal of feminine and spousal virtues and is known for her courage, dedication and purity. As per the ancient text of Ramayana considered sacred by people practicing Hindu religion, Lord Rama and Devi Sita are referred to as the perfect man and woman.
I hereby pray to Lord Rama and Goddess Sita, for the well being, love, happiness, strength, positive energy, prosperity, and success of my readers in their life. To please and evoke the powers of the Lord Rama and Mother Sita for the well-being of the world, I hereby recite the following mantra...

"Sita Ram Sita Ram Sita Ram Jai Sita Ram"

Table of Contents

Introduction...V

Keyword Index...VI, VII

Organisation Index..VIII, IX, X

Project Index...XI, XII, XIII, XIV, XV

Projects Section...1

Introduction

ProjectX India provides you with information on **137 projects** from **59** *sectors* of the economy. The aim of this e-publication is to track and provide information on upcoming projects, track progress of the ongoing projects, contracts awarded recently, and projects completed / commissioned. In order to facilitate b2b exchange, these project leads powered by the contact information can help the reader to explore further business opportunities at various levels. The business environment is highly challenging and information about projects in the nascent / conceptual stage can really help businesses to take the first mover advantage, prepare well in advance to grab the opportunity when it comes to the fore. This e-publication is just a small attempt to help the nation builders in their mission. If you keep reading, referring, and using the project information from this e-publication and the upcoming editions, you will be able to identify the right business opportunity for you.

"When you can't see any opportunity in an adverse environment, do not wait for it but take the initiative to create one."

I sincerely hope, you will find information provided in ProjectX India relevant for your business and help you to win more contracts and explore business opportunities.

Thank You and Happy Reading.

Keyword Index

A

Aerospace 2
aerospace laboratory 2
Agrochemicals 3
Agro Products 3
Aircraft 2
Alloys Wheels 6
Aluminium Extrusions 4
Aluminium Park 4
Automotive Components 5, 6
Aviation 2

B

Battery 6
Biorefineries 7
Bomb blankets 2
Breweries/Distilleries 7, 8
Bulk drug 9
Bullet proof vests 2

C

Captive generation plant 40
Captive power plant 11
Cement 9
Ceramic Wall Tiles 30
Chemicals 10, 11, 12, 13, 14, 15
Club House 51
Coal 15, 16, 17
Coal Mining 15, 16
Co-generation power plant 12
Construction 37, 39, 44, 51, 52, 53, 54, 55, 56, 57, 58, 59
Consultancy Services 17
Crane 18

D

Decorative Sheets 34
Defence 2, 18, 19
Defence Park 2
Dehumidifiers 19
Diesel Engine 20
distillery 7
drones 2
Drugs / Pharma 20, 21, 22, 23, 24
Dyes and Intermediates 25

E

Education 25
Electrical / Electronics 26, 27
Electrical Insulators 26
Ethanol 27, 28
Explosives 28

F

Fertilizers 29
Fitness Centre 51
Floor Tiles 30, 31
Forgings 31

G

Gas Exploration 38

H

Helicopter 18
helicopters 2
Hospitality 32
Housing 32
HVAC 33
Hydro Power 33

I

ICT 34

L

Laminated / Decorative Sheets 34
Lighting Devices 35
Lithium-Ion Battery 6

Keyword Index

M

Material Handling System 35
Metal Alloys 36
Metro Rail 37, 38
molasses based distillery 62
Molasses based Distillery 8
Molasses/grain based Distillery 8
Motor Vehicles Parts 5
Multi-level parking 4

O

Oil and Gas 38, 39, 40, 41
organic chemicals 44
Organic Chemicals 10, 11, 13, 14

P

Pesticide 3, 9, 11, 14, 41
Petrochemical 42
Pipes / Pipe Fittings 42, 43
Plastic Products 43
Plywood 34
Polymers 44
Power 44, 45, 46
Pre-engineered Bldg 37, 46

R

Railways 47, 48
Rapid Transit System 47
Real Estate 48, 49, 50, 51
Refinery 40
Renewable Energy 51
Roads/Highways/Bridges 52, 53, 54, 55, 56, 57, 58, 59

S

Sheet Metal parts 5
Simulators 2
Soda ash 12

Solar Energy 59, 60, 61, 62
specialty chemicals 9, 15
Specialty Chemicals 3, 11
Starch & Chemicals 3
Sugar 62, 63
Sugar Alcohol 63

T

Technical Textiles 64
Thermal power plant 26, 35, 45, 46
Tourism 64
Transmission 44, 45
Transport 65
Two Wheeler 5

U

Urban Development 65

V

Vitrified Tiles 30, 31

W

Waste Management 66
Water Treatment 66, 67, 68
Wax 68
Wheel Rim 6
Wind Energy 69
Wires and Cables 70

Click project number to access the respective project containing the keyword. Use Alt + Left arrow key to come back to the Keyword Index page.

Organisation Index

Organisation Name	Project Sno.
ABB Power Products and Systems India Limited (APPSIL)	77
Ace Mica Private Limited	66
Adani Green Energy Five Limited	135
Adani Green Energy Three Limited	136
Aditya Birla Power Composites Limited (ABPCL)	49
Aditya Industries	70
Airports Authority of India	5, 129
Aishwarya Avant Builders LLP	96
Alfa Mana Realtors Private Limited	95
Anand Developers	98
Anaven LLP	22
A-One Chemicals	17
Apicore Pharmaceuticals Private Limited	41
Ashirvad Pipes Private Limited	82
Askins Biofuels Private Limited	53
Banstag Life Sciences Limited	44
Benzochem Industries Private Limited	23
Bharat Coking Coal Limited	28
Bharat Dynamics Limited	35
Bharat Heavy Electricals Limited (BHEL)	50, 118, 119
Biocon Biologics India Limited	43
Bombardier Transportation India Private Limited	92
Cadila Healthcare Limited	38
Chemline India Limited	134
Chryso India Private Limited	24
Corel Pharma Chem Private Limited	85
Coromandel Sugars Limited	13
Crevita Granito Private Limited	59
Deepak Nitrite Limited	25
Department of Tourism, Govt of West Bengal	126
Department of Water Supply & Sanitation, Govt of Punjab	132
Department of Water Supply, Kanpur Nagar Nigam	133
Dhruv Consultancy Services Limited	32
Escorts Limited	37
Flowtech Chemicals Private Limited	26
Focus Energy Limited	79
Garg Inox Limited	137
Genesis Impex (India) Limited	69
Glen Industries Private Limited	84
Godavari Biorefineries Limited	11
Godavari Farm Chemical Industries Private Limited	80

Organisation Index

Organisation Name	Project Sno.
Greater Hyderabad Municipal Corporation (GHMC)	110
Greater Mohali Area Development Authority (GMADA)	128
Greater Noida Industrial Development Authority (GNIDA)	**112**
Gujarat Fluorochemicals Limited	52
Gujarat Organics Limited	16
Hindustan Zinc Limited	56
Indian Institute of Technology (IIT) Goa	48
Indo Autotech Limited	7
Italico Ceramic	58
Ittehad Buildcon	99
Izra Solar Energy Private Limited	117
J. Kumar Infraprojects Limited	71
Jaipur Development Authority (JDA)	109
Jakraya Sugar Limited	123
JBM Solar	116
Jharkhand Urban Infrastructure Development Company Limited (JUIDCO)	130
Jindal Aluminium Limited	6
Kasyap Sweetners Limited	124
Keltech Energies Limited	54
Klassic Wheels Limited	9
Krishnum Dyes & Intermediate Private Limited	47
Kwality Pharmaceuticals Limited	42
Malbros International Private Limited	14
Meghalaya Power Generation Corporation Limited (MePGCL)	64
Metalman Micro Turners	8
Ministry of Defence, Govt of India	34
Ministry of Road Transport & Highways (MoRT&H)	104 - 108, 111 - 114
Mumbai Metro Rail Corporation (MMRC)	62
Mumbai Metro Rail Corporation (MMRC)	72
Mumbai Metropolitan Region Development Authority (MMRDA)	73
Municipal Corporation of Greater Mumbai	33, 90
Nalco Water India Limited	27
National Highway & Infrastructure Development Corporation Limited (NHIDCL)	102 - 103
National Highways Authority of India (NHAI)	107
Navitasys India Private Limited	10
Nayara Energy Limited	78
Nec Real Estate Private Limited	94
New Town Kolkata Development Authority (NKDA)	67, 120
Niser Industries	20
NLC India Limited	89
NTPC Limited	30, 36, 63, 65, 68, 88, 131

Organisation Index

Organisation Name	Project Sno.
Numaligarh Refinery Limited (NRL)	75
Oil India Limited	76
Om Sahil Solitaire Builders	97
Ozone Life Science	39
Pragna Pharma Private Limited	4
Provenance Land Private Limited	61
Public Works Department, Govt of West Bengal	115
Rail Land Development Authority (RLDA)	91
Reliance Industries Limited (RIL)	81
RGPPL (Ratnagiri Gas and Power Private Limited.)	83
Rural Works Division, Govt of Arunachal Pradesh	101
Salasar Techno Engineering Limited	86
Saurashtra Chemicals (Division of Nirma Limited)	21
SGR Laboratories Private Limited	46
Shiraguppi Sugar Works Limited	12
Shivneri Sugars Limited	122
Singareni Collieries Company Limited (SCCL)	31
Solar Energy Corporation of India (SECI)	100
Sona Blw Precision Forgings Limited	60
South Central Railway (SCR)	93
Springway Mining Private Limited	15
SRF Limited	19
Steel Authority of India Limited	29
Sterlite Power Transmission Limited	87
Strata Geosystems (India) Private Limited	125
Tata Power Strategic Engineering Division	1
The Fertilizers and Chemicals Travancore (FACT) Limited	55
Tirumangalam Municipality	127
Tirupati Starch & Chemicals Limited	3
Titan Aviation and Aerospace India Limited (TAAIL)	2
US Amino Private Limited	45
Valiant Organics Limited	18
Varda Life Science LLP	40
Vedanta Limited (Division Cairn Oil & Gas)	74
Vicon Ceramic Private Limited	57
West Bengal Power Development Corporation Limited (WBPDCL)	51, 121

Project Index

Sector / Project Title	Project Sno.	Page No.
Aerospace		
Defence contract for Tata Power	1	2
Aero and Defence Park	2	2
Agro Products		
Maize Husk unit at Dhar	3	3
Agrochemicals		
Expansion of pesticides plant at Dahej	4	3
Airport		
Multi-level parking project at Pune airport	5	4
Aluminium		
Aluminium Extrusions plant at Angul	6	4
Automotive Components		
Motor Vehicles Parts unit at Ahmedabad	7	5
Two Wheeler Frame Body unit at Rewari	8	5
Alloys Wheels unit at Ahmednagar	9	6
Battery		
Lithium-Ion Battery Pack For Mobile unit at Gurugram	10	6
Breweries/Distilleries		
Expansion of distillery unit in Bagalkot district	11	7
Establishment of 120 KLPD molasses based distillery at Kagwad	12	7
Molasses/grain based Distillery at Mandya	13	8
160 KLPD Molasses based Distillery at Shahjahanpur	14	8
Cement		
Cement unit at Damoh	15	9
Chemicals		
Expansion of bulk drug intermediates mfg capacity at	16	9
Expansion of synthetic organic chemical manufacturing capacity	17	10
O-Cumidine unit at Bharuch	18	10
Expansion of chemical and power plant at Dahej	19	11
Expansion of synthetic organic chemical manufacturing capacity	20	11
Modernisation and expansion of Soda ash facility at Porbandar	21	12
Expansion of Monochloro Acetic Acid (MCA) at Valsad plant	22	12
Expansion of chemical intermediates mfg capacity at Buldhana	23	13
Synthetic Organic chemicals unit expansion at Turbhe	24	13
Establishment of Pesticide specific intermediates unit at Roha	25	14
Expansion of chemical mfg unit at PACL campus	26	14
Capacity augmentation of specialty chemicals at Konanagar	27	15
Coal		
Cluster VII Coal Mining Project in Jharkhand	28	15
Jitpur Underground Colliery project	29	16

Project Index

Sector / Project Title	Project Sno.	Page No.
Kerendari Coal Mining Project	30	16
Prakasham Khani Opencast Coal Mine Project	31	17
Consultancy Services		
Consultancy projects for Meghalaya roads	32	17
Crane		
15/5 Ton crane at Bhandup Complex	33	18
Defence		
Helicopter manufacturing unit in India	34	18
Supply order from Indian Air Force	35	19
Dehumidifiers	36	
Supply of Dehumidifiers at Kayamkulam	36	19
Diesel Engine		
Diesel Engines unit at Rajkot	37	20
Drugs / Pharma		
Capacity expansion of bulk drug unit at Ankleshwar	38	20
Bulk Drug & Intermediates Manufacturing Unit at Ankleshwar	39	21
Bulk drug mfg unit at Ankleshwar	40	22
Expansion of bulk drug unit at Vadodara	41	23
Cefaclor Oral Suspension unit at Kangra	42	23
Human insulin unit at Bengaluru	43	24
API manufacturing plant at SAS Nagar	44	23
Expansion of bulk drugs and intermediate unit at Udaipur	45	24
Bulk Drugs and Drug Intermediates unit in Suryapet	46	24
Dyes and Intermediates		
Dyes and Intermediates manufacturing project in Churu	47	25
Education		
IIT Campus at Guleli	48	25
Electrical / Electronics		
Electrical Insulators unit at Panchamahal	49	26
400 kV post insulators for Panki TPS	50	26
Electrical works for G+6 storey building at Sagardighi	51	27
Ethanol	105	
Ethanol unit at Belgaum	53	27
Ethanol unit at Bharuch	52	28
Explosives		
Expansion of explosive products mfg capacity at Nagpur	54	28
Fertilizers		
Capacity Enhancement of Complex Fertiliser Production at Ambalamedu	55	29
Greenfield Ammonium Phosphate Fertilizer Complex at Biliya	56	29
Floor Tiles		
Ceramic wall tiles at Morbi	57	30

Project Index

Sector / Project Title	Project Sno.	Page No.
Tiles unit at Morbi	58	30
Vitrified Tiles unit at Morbi	59	31
Forgings		
Driveline Aggregates unit at Gurugram	60	31
Hospitality		
Four Seasons Private Residences Phase - 1	61	32
Housing		
Multi-storey buildings at Girgaum-Kalbadevi	62	32
HVAC		
Air Conditioning work for hospital extension bldg at Unchahar	63	33
Hydro Power		
Riangdo Small Hydro Power Project	64	33
ICT		
Centralised monitoring analytical tool for solar plant at Mandsaur	65	34
Laminated / Decorative Sheets		
Laminated and Decorative sheets unit at Gandhinagar	66	34
Lighting Devices		
Supply and installation of Solar studs in New Kolkata	67	35
Material Handling System		
Dry ash handling system for Bongaigaon TPP	68	35
Metal Alloys		
Lead Ingots unit at Valsad	69	36
M S Ingot unit at Sirmur	70	36
Metro Rail		
Mumbai metro line 7 elevated duct contract	71	37
Mumbai metro project line 3	72	37
Mumbai metro project line 7	73	38
Oil and Gas		
Expansion of offshore and onshore oil and gas production in KG basin	74	38
Numaligarh refinery expansion project	75	39
Drilling and testing of hydrocarbons in Tinsukia	76	39
220/33 kilovolt gas-insulated switchgear (GIS) substation contract from IOCL	77	40
Expansion of refinery at Vadinar	78	40
Expansion of existing 17 production wells in Jaisalmer	79	41
Pesticides		
Pesticide unit at Pochampalli	80	41
Petrochemical		
Expansiion of petrochemical manufacturing capacity at Vadodara	81	42
Pipes / Pipe Fittings		
PVC Pipes unit at Bengaluru	82	42

Project Index

Sector / Project Title	Project Sno.	Page No.
Procurement of MS Pipes for RGPPL	83	43
Plastic Products		
Plastic Containers unit at Paradeep	84	43
Polymers		
Acrylate polymers unit in Mehsana	85	44
Power		
220 & 66 KV Transmission lines in Yamuna Nagar	86	44
Gurgaon Palwal Transmission Project (GPTL)	87	45
Expansion of Talcher TPS	88	45
Thermal power plant at Tareikela	89	46
Pre-engineered Bldg		
Three-storey isolation wards at Kasturba Gandhi Hospital	90	46
Railways		
Redevelopment of Tirupati railway station	91	47
Regional Rapid Transit System (RRTS) contract	92	47
Cherlapally Railway Terminal development	93	48
Real Estate		
Tourist complex at Bengaluru	94	48
A M Residency project at Mazgaon	95	49
Avant Heritage project at Jogeshwari	96	49
Om Sahil Solitaire Project	97	50
Green Country Phase-II project	98	50
S K Valley project at Thane	99	51
Renewable Energy		
400 MW RE power contract award	100	51
Roads/Highways/Bridges		
Miao to Vijoynagar road project	101	52
Widening of Dokmoka Loring Thepi Section	102	52
Widening of Loring Thepi Ganapath Gaur Gaon Section	103	53
Widening of Ibrampura to Tekkalkote road section	106	53
Delhi-Mumbai Expressway project	107	54
Sodala elevated road project in Jaipur	109	54
Construction of link roads connecting highways in Hyderabad	110	55
Widening of section from Bharthana Chowk to Kodarkoot	111	55
Bridge across Hindon river	112	56
Strengthening of road on NH-309	113	56
Majerhat bridge project	115	57
Balance work of Bridges on Theog Kotkhai Hatkoti section	209	57
Widening of Kirshal-Chaura road section	222	58
Solar Energy		
100 MW solar projects across the country	116	58

Project Index

Sector / Project Title	Project Sno.	Page No.
Solar power unit at Belgaum	117	59
360 KWP Solar System at VTU Belagavi	118	59
Type testing of solar PV modules	119	60
1 MW canal top solar project at Bagjola	120	60
10 MW of grid-connected floating solar project at Sagardighi	121	61
Sugar		
Sugar factory in Kopergaon	122	61
Expansion of sugar factory at Watwate	123	62
Sugar Alcohol		
Sorbitol Solution unit at Dhar	124	62
Technical Textiles		
Technical Textile unit at Valsad	125	63
Tourism		
Bhorer Alo tourism works	126	63
Transport		
New Bus Stand in Tirumangalam	127	64
Urban Development		
GMADA to take up internal works in Mohali	128	64
Waste Management		
Zero Waste Management Plant at Imphal	129	65
Water Treatment		
9.5 MLD water treatment plant in Jharkhand	130	65
O&M of water treatment plant of NTPC Mouda plant	131	66
14 MLD Water Treatment plant in Gurdaspur	132	66
Submersible system for Benajhber WTP	133	67
Wax		
Laminating Wax unit at Sonipat	134	67
Wind Energy		
300 MW Wind Energy unit at Kutch	135	68
Wind Energy unit at Kutch	136	68
Wires and Cables		
S S wire unit at Jhajjar	137	69

You can share your project, contract, tender details to feature in ProjectX India.

Email your project details to
Editor@ProjectXIndia.com

PROJECT X
India

137 PROJECTS IN THIS ISSUE

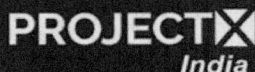

Sno. 1	Project Stage: Contract Award
Sector: Aerospace	Location: Nationwide

Project Name / Title	Defence contract for Tata Power

Details: Tata Power Strategic Engineering Division is a unit of Tata Power, a diversified company of the Tata Group. The company has recently bagged a defence contract comprising the modernization of air field infrastructure (MAFI) for Indian Air Force (IAF), Indian Navy (IN) and Indian Coast Guard (ICG) as part of the second phase.

Est. Value (Rs. Cr)	1200
Organisation	Tata Power Strategic Engineering Division

Contact Details: Praveer Sinha, CEO & Managing Director, 42 Off Saki - Vihar Road, Andheri (East) Mumbai - 400072. Phone: 022-67513601, 67513600, Fax: 67513638, Email: marketing@tatapowersed.com

---

Sno. 2	Project Stage: Conceptual/Planning
Sector: Aerospace	Location: *Jhansi* Uttar Pradesh

Project Name / Title	Aero and Defence Park

Details: Titan Aviation plans to set up Aero and Defence Park spread over 6,000 acre in Jhansi along the Defence Corridor in the under-developed Bundelkhand region. The industrial park will be developed in four phases with the collaboration of Ukrainian Companies. The park will host an aviation university, aerospace laboratory, simulators for airbus, Boeing as well as Russian helicopters, an advance maintenance center for aircraft and last-stage manufacturing unit of drones, bullet proof vests and bomb blankets.

Est. Value (Rs. Cr)	37000
Organisation	Titan Aviation and Aerospace India Limited (TAAIL)

Contact Details: K Giri Kumar, Chairman and CEO, Flat No. 302, Keerthi Villa, Machabollaram, Secunderabad, Telangana - 500010. Phone: 040-7861901, 27861902, 27861903, Fax: 27861904, Email: office.ind@taail.com

Sno. 3		Project Stage: Conceptual/Planning
Sector: Agro Products		Location: *Dhar* Madhya Pradesh
Project Name / Title	Maize Husk unit at Dhar	
Details: The company has decided to set up Maize Husk unit at Dhar Madhya Pradesh. The unit will have 8050 Mt capacity.		
Est. Value (Rs. Cr)	NA	
Organisation	Tirupati Starch & Chemicals Limited	
Contact Details: Amit Modi, Managing Director, Shree Ram Chambers, 1st Floor, 12 Agrawal Nagar, Indore, Madhya Pradesh-452001. Phone: 0731-2405001-2-3, Fax: 2405000, E-Mail: tirupati@tirupatistarch.com		

Sno. 4		Project Stage: Project Update
Sector: Agrochemicals		Location: *Bharuch* Gujarat
Project Name / Title	Expansion of pesticides plant at Dahej	
Details: Pragna Pharma is implementing expansion of Pesticides Intermediates & Specialty Chemicals unit in existing Inorganic Chemicals unit at Plot No. D2/CH/224, GIDC Industrial Estate, Dahej-II, Taluk Vagra, District Bharuch. The company has recently sought amendment in the environment clearance issued earlier.		
Est. Value (Rs. Cr)	NA	
Organisation	Pragna Pharma Private Limited	
Contact Details: Jigneshkumar Kalidas Patel, Director, Plot No. 1210, GIDC, Ankleshwar-393002, Dist: Bharuch, Gujarat. Phone: (02646) 238106, Mobile: 9723812606, Email: jignesh@pragnapharma.com		

Sno. 5		Project Stage: Under Implementation
Sector: Airport		Location: *Pune* Maharashtra
Project Name / Title	Multi-level parking project at Pune airport	
Details: Airports Authoriy of India is implementing the 1,000-car Multi-level parking project at Pune airport. The work will be carried out in two phases. Pebbles Infrastructure, the project contractor has resumed construction work as part of Phase-I.		
Est. Value (Rs. Cr)	120	
Organisation	Airports Authority of India	
Contact Details: Srinivas Rao, Interim Director, Civil Enclave Pune Airport, Lohegaon, Pune, Maharashtra. Phone: 020-26683232, Fax: 26685599, Email: apdpune@aai.aero		

Sno. 6		Project Stage: Conceptual/Planning
Sector: Aluminium		Location: *Angul* Odisha
Project Name / Title	Aluminium Extrusions plant at Angul	
Details: Jindal Aluminium Limited plans to set up 75,000 MT / annum Aluminium Extrusions plant at Angul Aluminium Park, Angul. SLSWCA in-principle approved the proposal on		
Est. Value (Rs. Cr)	500	
Organisation	Jindal Aluminium Limited	
Contact Details: Pragun Jindal Khaitan, Managing Director, Jindal Nagar, Tumkur Road, Bengaluru 560 073 Phone: 080-23715555,Fax: 23713333, E-mail: jindal@jindalaluminium.com		

Sno. 7	**Project Stage:** Conceptual/Planning
Sector: Automotive Components	**Location:** *Ahmedabad* Gujarat

Project Name / Title	Motor Vehicles Parts unit at Ahmedabad

Details: Indo Autotech Limited plans to set up Motor Vehicles Parts and Sheet Metal parts unit at Ahmedabad in the state of Gujarat. The unit will have 7200000 Nos capacity.

Est. Value (Rs. Cr)	NA
Organisation	Indo Autotech Limited

Contact Details: 1) Anand Jain, Managing Director, Plot No.332-338, Mujesar Police Station, Sector-24, Faridabad, Haryana - 121005. Phone: 129-4020837, Email: anandjain@indoautotech.com, Website: www.indoautotech.com 2) Vikram Gupta, Chief General Manager Design & Development, Email: vikram@indoautotech.com

---

Sno. 8	**Project Stage:** Conceptual/Planning
Sector: Automotive Components	**Location:** *Rewari* Haryana

Project Name / Title	Two Wheeler Frame Body unit at Rewari

Details: Metalman Auto Private Limited's group company plans to undertake manufacturing of Two Wheeler Frame Body And Parts unit at Rewari, Haryana. The unit will have 1460000 Pieces capacity.

Est. Value (Rs. Cr)	NA
Organisation	Metalman Micro Turners

Contact Details: Vivek Narang, Co-Founder & Managing Director, Khewat No.64, Khatoni No. 65, Akera Road, Village Kapriwas, Dharuhera, Rewari Haryana-123106. Phone: 011-41881755, Email: narangv@gmail.com, info@mmtonweb.com

Sno. 9		Project Stage: Conceptual/Planning	
Sector: Automotive Components		Location: *Ahmednagar* **Maharashtra**	
Project Name / Title	Alloys Wheels unit at Ahmednagar		
Details: Klassic Wheels Limited plans to manufacture Wheel Rim For Two Wheeler, Three Wheeler, and Four Wheeler including Alloys Wheels unit at Ahmednagar, Maharashtra. The unit will have 1000000 Nos capacity.			
Est. Value (Rs. Cr)	NA		
Organisation	Klassic Wheels Limited		
Contact Details: 1) Sunil Munot, Managing Director 2) K Gopinathan, G.M (Sales & Marketing), E-7 & E-8 Nagar, Manmad Rd, MIDC, Ahmednagar, Maharashtra - 414111. Phone: 0241-2779415, Mobile: 9850954549, Email: info@klassicwheels.com			

Sno. 10		Project Stage: Conceptual/Planning
Sector: Battery		Location: *Gurugram* **Haryana**
Project Name / Title	Lithium-Ion Battery Pack For Mobile unit at Gurugram	
Details: The company has decided to set up Lithium-Ion Battery Pack For Mobile unit at Gurugram, Haryana. The unit will have 31920000 Pcs capacity.		
Est. Value (Rs. Cr)	NA	
Organisation	Navitasys India Private Limited	
Contact Details: Shirish Prasad, Managing Director, Plot No.32, Sector-5, Phase-Ii, Hsiidc, Industri- Al, Growth Centre, Bawal, Rewari, Haryana-123501. gaurav.garg@nvtpower.com		

Sno. 11		Project Stage: Conceptual/Planning
Sector: Breweries/Distilleries		Location: *Bagalkot District* **Andhra Pradesh**
Project Name / Title	Expansion of distillery unit in Bagalkot district	
Details: Godavari Biorefineries Ltd plans to undertake expansion of distillery unit from 320 KLPD to 400 KLPD at Sy. No. 16 & 17 of Saidapur Village, Sy. No.45 Sameerwadi Mudhol Taluk, Bagalkot District. Environmental clearance is sought.		
Est. Value (Rs. Cr)	133.2	
Organisation	Godavari Biorefineries Limited	
Contact Details: 1) C.P.Poojari, AGM (Alchohol & Chemical), Unity Building, Tower Block, 4th Floor, J C Road, Bengaluru - 560002. Phone: 080-22236479, Fax: 22219103, Email: cpoojari@somaiya.com 2) Suhas Uttam Godage, General Manager, At post Sameerwadi, Tal: Mudhol, Dist: Bagalkot-587316. Phone: 08350-260046, Fax: 260046, Email: suhas@somaiya.com		

Sno. 12		Project Stage: Conceptual/Planning
Sector: Breweries/Distilleries		Location: *Belgaum* **Karnataka**
Project Name / Title	Establishment of 120 KLPD molasses based distillery at Kagwad	
Details: Shiraguppi Sugar Works Ltd plans to undertake expansion of sugar factory output from 4000 TCD to 10,000 TCD, Co-gen plant from 15 MW to 60MW, and Establishment of 120 KLPD molasses based distillery at Kagwad, Tal: Athani, District: Belgaum. Environment clearance is sought.		
Est. Value (Rs. Cr)	300	
Organisation	Shiraguppi Sugar Works Limited	
Contact Details: Dr Ramesh P Doddannavar, Managing Director, Kagwad village,Athani Tq.Belgaum Dist, Karnataka-590016.Phone: 0831-2461231, Email: hra@sswlsugars.com		

Sno. 13	**Project Stage:** Conceptual/Planning
Sector: Breweries/Distilleries	**Location:** *Mandya District* **Karnataka**
Project Name / Title	Molasses/grain based Distillery at Mandya
Details: Coromandel Sugars Limited plans to set up Molasses/grain based Distillery (45 KLPD), Co-generation Plant (30MW) and Captive Power Plant (1.5MW) at Sf. No.51, Village Makavalli, Tehsil Krishnarajpet, District: Mandya, Karnataka. The company has sought amendment in the environmental clearance issued earlier.	
Est. Value (Rs. Cr)	NA
Organisation	Coromandel Sugars Limited
Contact Details: T.S. Raghupathy, Director, Coromandel Towers, 93, Karpagam Avenue Santhome High Road R.A. Puram, Chennai - 600028. Phone: 044 28520455, Email: cpk@indiacements.co.in	

Sno. 14	**Project Stage:** Conceptual/Planning
Sector: Breweries/Distilleries	**Location:** *Shahjahanpur District* **Uttar Pradesh**
Project Name / Title	160 KLPD Molasses based Distillery at Shahjahanpur
Details: Malbros International has proposed 160 KLPD Molasses based Distillery along with 7.0 MW co-generation power plant at Village Bhatiyura Prathipur, Tehsil Tilhar, District: Shahjahanpur, Uttar Pradesh. Environmental clearance is awaited.	
Est. Value (Rs. Cr)	225
Organisation	Malbros International Private Limited
Contact Details: Pawan, Bansal, CAO, 40-A, N.A.Road, Punjabi Bagh, New Delhi, Delhi. Phone: 011-47012635, Fax: 47012635, Email: malbros@ymail.com	

Sno. 15	Project Stage: Conceptual/Planning
Sector: Cement	Location: *Damoh* Madhya Pradesh

Project Name / Title	Cement unit at Damoh
Details: Springway Mining Private Limited plans to manufacture all types of Cements at Damoh Madhya Pradesh. The unit will have 2200000 MetrIc Tons capacity.	
Est. Value (Rs. Cr)	109
Organisation	Springway Mining Private Limited
Contact Details: Sushil Mansukhani, Director, Mcleod House, 1st Floor 3, Netaji Subhas Road, Kolkata West Bengal-700001. Phone: 0751-2340708, Email: springwaypvtltd@gmail.com	

Sno. 16	Project Stage: Conceptual/Planning
Sector: Chemicals	Location: *Ankleshwar* Gujarat

Project Name / Title	Expansion of bulk drug intermediates mfg capacity at
Details: Gujarat Organics Limited plans to undertake expansion of existing bulk drug intermediates, pesticide specific intermediates & specialty chemicals manufacturing unit located at Ankleshwar, District Bharuch. Environmental clearance is sought.	
Est. Value (Rs. Cr)	6.45
Organisation	Gujarat Organics Limited
Contact Details: 1) Hasit Ashwin Dani, 3 A, Barodawala Mansion, 81 Dr. A.B. Road, Worli, Mumbai - 400018. Phone: 022-43625500, Fax: 24974886 2) Malek M.K, Manager Production & EHS, Plot No. 127/1 G.I.D.C. Industrial Estate, Ankleshwar, Gujarat - 393002. Phone: 02646-222170, Fax: 251787, Email: golank@gujaratorganics.com	

Sno. 17	Project Stage: Conceptual/Planning
Sector: Chemicals	Location: Bharuch Gujarat

Project Name / Title	Expansion of synthetic organic chemical manufacturing capacity

Details: A-One Chemicals is seeking environmental clearance for Manufacturing of Synthetic Organic Chemicals (Pigments) Expansion Project, located at Plot No. A-1/ 4701 & 4702, GIDC Estate, Ankleshwar, Dist:-Bharuch, Gujarat.

Est. Value (Rs. Cr)	5
Organisation	A-One Chemicals

Contact Details: 1) Ghanshyam Patel, Director, Plot No. A-1/4701,4702, GIDC Estate, Ankleshwar, Bharuch, Gujarat -393002. Phone: 079-26468261, Email: gbp@aonechemicals.com 2) 302, Shanti House, Off C.G. Road, Navrangpura, Ahmedabad - 380009, Gujarat. Phone: 079-26468261 , 26468262, 9904045115, 9825845515, Fax: 26468200, Email: aone@aonechemicals.com

Sno. 18	Project Stage: Conceptual/Planning
Sector: Chemicals	Location: Bharuch Gujarat

Project Name / Title	O-Cumidine unit at Bharuch

Details: The company has decided to set up Metanilic Acid, O-Cumidine unit at Bharuch Gujarat. The unit will have 30000 Mts capacity.

Est. Value (Rs. Cr)	NA
Organisation	Valiant Organics Limited

Contact Details: 1) Arvind Chheda, Managing Director, 109, Udyog Kshetra, 1st Floor, Mulund Goregaon Link Road, Mulund (W), Mumbai - 400080. Phone: 022-67976683, Email: info@valiantorganics.com

Sno. 19		Project Stage: Under Implementation
Sector: Chemicals		Location: Bharuch District Gujarat
Project Name / Title	Expansion of chemical and power plant at Dahej	
Details: SRF Limited plans to carry out expansion of Specialty Chemicals, Pesticide, Fluoro Chemicals & Captive power plant in the existing unit located at Dahej. The company has sought amendment in the environment clearance given so far.		
Est. Value (Rs. Cr)	4800	
Organisation	SRF Limited	
Contact Details: 1) Ashish Bharat Ram, CEO & MD 2) Dhananjay Ranade, Senior Vice President & Head of Works, Plot No. D-2/1,Village: Suva, GIDC Phase II, Dahej, Taluka Vagra, District: Bharuch, Gujarat. Phone:02641-289201, Email: dhananjay.ranade@srf.com 3) Nitika Dhawan, Head of Corporate Communications, Email: nitikadhawan19@gmail.com, nitika.dhawan@srf.com		

Sno. 20		Project Stage: Conceptual/Planning
Sector: Chemicals		Location: Morbi District Gujarat
Project Name / Title	Expansion of synthetic organic chemical manufacturing capacity	
Details: Niser Industries plans to undertake the expansion of Synthetic Organic Chemicals (Resin manufacturing unit) in the existing unit at Survey No.: 350, Paiki 3, Plot No. 7, Village: Bagathala, Taluka & District: Morbi, Gujarat. Environmental Clearance is sought.		
Est. Value (Rs. Cr)	1.4	
Organisation	Niser Industries	
Contact Details: Parag Zalaria, Partner, Plot No.7, Survey No. 350-3, Village. Bagathia, T.D. Morbi, Gujarat - 363641. Phone: 9099059259, Email: Niser.morbi@gmail.com		

Sno. 21	Project Stage: Conceptual/Planning
Sector: Chemicals	Location: *Porbandar* Gujarat

Project Name / Title	Modernisation and expansion of Soda ash facility at Porbandar
Details: Saurashtra Chemicals proposes to undertake the expansion through modernization in existing production capacity of facility of Soda Ash (from 35,720 MT/M to 45020 MT/M) and Co-generation power plant (from 20 MW to 40 MW) in existing production facility at Birlasagar, Porbandar, Gujarat. Environmental clearance is sought.	
Est. Value (Rs. Cr)	151.5
Organisation	Saurashtra Chemicals (Division of Nirma Limited)
Contact Details: 1) Hiren K. Patel, Managing Director, Nirma House Ashram Road, Ahmedabad, Gujarat-380009. Phone: 079-27549000, Fax: 27546603/05, Email: info@nirma.co.in 2) Ashish Desai, Project Coordinator, Phone: 079-27549319, Email: mines@nirma.co.in	

Sno. 22	Project Stage: Conceptual/Planning
Sector: Chemicals	Location: *Valsad District* Gujarat

Project Name / Title	Expansion of Monochloro Acetic Acid (MCA) at Valsad plant
Details: Anaven LLP plans to undertake expansion of Monochloro Acetic Acid (MCA) plant at Village Atul, District Valsad, Gujarat. Environmental Clearance is awaited.	
Est. Value (Rs. Cr)	187.5
Organisation	Anaven LLP
Contact Details: 1) Thirukonda Gopi Kannan Rengachari, Body Corporate DP Nominee 2) Purvesh, Deputy Manager, At & PO Atul, Dist. Valsad, Gujarat - 396020. Phone: 02632-233261, Email: purvesh_shroff@atul.co.in	

Sno. 23	Project Stage: Conceptual/Planning
Sector: Chemicals	Location: *Buldhana District* **Maharashtra**

Project Name / Title	Expansion of chemical intermediates mfg capacity at Buldhana

Details: Benzochem Industries Pvt Ltd plans to undertake the expansion in manufacturing production capacity of existing chemical intermediates located at Plot No.B-26,27,14,15, Dasarkhed MIDC, Talkuka Malkapur, District Buldhana. Environmental Clearance is sought.

Est. Value (Rs. Cr)	12
Organisation	Benzochem Industries Private Limited

Contact Details: 1) Surendra Mohatta, Chairman and Managing Director, 26/28 A, Cawasji Patel Street, Fort, Mumbai - 400001. Phone: 022-43555888, Email: smohatta@hotmail.com 2) Sunil Nawal, Director (Operations), Email: nawal@benzochem.co.in 3) Pralhad Narayan Zope, Director, Phone: 7267-7267262341, Email: zope@benzochem.co.in,

Sno. 24	Project Stage: Conceptual/Planning
Sector: Chemicals	Location: *Navi Mumbai* **Maharashtra**

Project Name / Title	Synthetic Organic chemicals unit expansion at Turbhe

Details: Chryso India Private Limited plans to implement expansion project for Manufacturing of Synthetic Organic Chemicals (Acrylic Co-Polymers for Construction Chemicals & Other Industries) at Plot No.D-30/7, TTC Industrial Area MIDC, Turbhe, Navi Mumbai (Maharashtra). Environmental clearance is sought.

Est. Value (Rs. Cr)	7.8
Organisation	Chryso India Private Limited

Contact Details: 1) Rajiv Upadhyay, Managing Director, Email: Rajiv.Upadhyay@chryso.com 2) Anirban Majumder, AVP, D 30/7, TTC Industrial Area, MIDC Industrial Area, Turbhe, Navi Mumbai, Maharashtra 400706. Phone: 022-27685991, Email: anirban.majumder@chryso.com

Tracking Projects for your business

Sno. 25	Project Stage: Conceptual/Planning
Sector: Chemicals	Location: *Raigad District* **Maharashtra**

Project Name / Title	Establishment of Pesticide specific intermediates unit at Roha

Details: Deepak Nitrite Limited has proposed establishment of Pesticide specific intermediates & Synthetic Organic Chemicals Manufacturing Facility at Plot No 53A, MIDC Roha, Dist- Raigad in the state of Maharashtra. Environmental clearance is sought.

Est. Value (Rs. Cr)	150
Organisation	Deepak Nitrite Limited

Contact Details: 1) D.C. Mehta, Chairman & Managing Director, Aaditya – I, Chhani Road, Vadodara – 390024. Gujarat. Phone: 0265-2765200, 3960200, Fax: 2765344, Email: dcmehta@deepaknitrite.com 2) Praveen Desai, Site Head, Phone: 0219-4263550

Tracking Projects for your business

Sno. 26	Project Stage: Conceptual/Planning
Sector: Chemicals	Location: *Ropar District* **Punjab**

Project Name / Title	Expansion of chemical mfg unit at PACL campus

Details: Flowtech Chemicals Private Limited plans to undertake expansion of Chemical Manufacturing unit located at PACL Campus, Industrial Area, Naya Nangal, District- Ropar, Punjab. Environmental Clearance is sought.

Est. Value (Rs. Cr)	NA
Organisation	Flowtech Chemicals Private Limited

Contact Details: 1) S S Dahiya, Director, PACL Campus, Industrial Area, Naya Nangal, District- Ropar, Punjab-140126. Phone: 0172-4669295, Email: flowtechchemicals1@gmail.com 2) Jatin Dahiya, 314-15 PP Towers, Netaji Subhash Place, Pitampura, Delhi-110034. Phone: 011-47049211, Mobile: 9899234211, Email: jatin.dahiya@flowtechgroup.in

Sno. 27	**Project Stage:** Conceptual/Planning
Sector: Chemicals	**Location:** *Hooghly District* **West Bengal**
Project Name / Title	Capacity augmentation of specialty chemicals at Konanagar

Details: Nalco Water India Limited plans to undertake the capacity augmentation of specialty chemicals from 11,000 to 22,000 TPA within the existing plat at Konnagar, Hooghly District in the state of West Bengal. Environmental clearance is pending.

Est. Value (Rs. Cr)	10
Organisation	Nalco Water India Limited

Contact Details: 1) Mukund Vasudevan, Managing Director, S. No. 238/239, Quadra 1, Panchshil, Magarpatta City Road, Sade Satra Nali, Pune - 411028. Phone: 020-66594000, Fax: 6659 4380, Email: mukund.vasudevan@ecolab.com 2) Jaideep Gupta, Plant Manager, No. 1, Lenin Sarani P.O. Konnagar, Dist : Hooghly West Bengal - 712235. Phone: 033-66801025. Email: jgupta@nalco.com.

Sno. 28	**Project Stage:** Under Implementation
Sector: Coal	**Location:** *Dhanbad District* **Jharkhand**
Project Name / Title	Cluster VII Coal Mining Project in Jharkhand

Details: Bharat Coking Coal Limited is undertaking expansion of Cluster VII Coal Mining Project from 8.16 MTPA to 11.42 MTPA in mine lease area of 2127.70 ha, located in Jharia Coalfields, District Dhanbad in the state of Jharkhand. The expansion got the environmental clearance in 2018. The company has recently sought an amendment for Approval of Revision of Calendar Program/Production Schedule of Cluster VII. The EAC after deliberation has deferred the proposal.

Est. Value (Rs. Cr)	NA
Organisation	Bharat Coking Coal Limited

Contact Details: J S Mahapatra, General Manager, Western Jharia Area, Moonidih PO: Moonidih, District – Dhanbad, Jharkhand – 828129. Phone: 0326-2273445 / 09470596225,Fax: 2273445.

Sno. 29	**Project Stage:** Project Update
Sector: Coal	**Location:** *Dhanbad District* **Jharkhand**

Project Name / Title	Jitpur Underground Colliery project

Details: Steel Authority of India is implementing the Jitpur Underground Colliery (0.6 (Normative) / 0.7 (Peak) MTPA in an ML area of 163.69 Ha, located Jitpur in District Dhanbad of Jharkhand state. Environment clearance is pending.

Est. Value (Rs. Cr)	222.69
Organisation	Steel Authority of India Limited

Contact Details: 1) Anil Kumar Chaudhary, Chairman, Ispat Bhawan, Lodi Road, New Delhi - 110003. Phone: 011-24367282, 24300100, Email: Chairman.sail@sail.in 2) Chitranjan Choudhary, GM (C&J), Collieries Division, Chasnalla, Jharkhand - 828135. Phone: 0326-2385004, Email: gmchasnalla@gmail.com

Sno. 30	**Project Stage:** Under Implementation
Sector: Coal	**Location:** *Hazaribagh* **Jharkhand**

Project Name / Title	Kerendari Coal Mining Project

Details: NTPC Limited is implementing the Kerendari 'A' Coal Mining Project of 6 MTPA peak capacity in mine lease area of 654 ha of M/s NTPC Limited located in villages Pandu, Tarhessa, Kabed, Pagar, Basaria and Lochar, Tehsil-Kerendari, District Hazaribagh in North Karanpura Coalfields. The company request for an amendment in environmental clearance for the project was turned down in April 2020. The amendment was related to transportation of coal.

Est. Value (Rs. Cr)	899.47
Organisation	NTPC Limited

Contact Details: 1) Gurdeep Singh, Chairman and Managing Director, NTPC Bhawan, SCOPE Complex, Institutional Area, Lodhi Road, New Delhi - 110003. Phone: 011 24360044, 24387000, Fax: 24361018, Email: cmd@ntpc.co.in, ntpccc@ntpc.co.in 2) S.K. Roy, Director (Projects), Phone: 011 24361090

Sno. 31	Project Stage: Conceptual/Planning
Sector: Coal	Location: Bhadradri District Telangana

Project Name / Title	Prakasham Khani Opencast Coal Mine Project

Details: SCCL plans to take up Prakasham Khani Opencast Coal Mine (Amalgamation of Manuguru OC II Expansion & Manuguru OC IV Extension) of 9.75 MTPA capacity in mine lease area of 2402.40 ha. (2214.84 ha is Forest Land and 187.56 ha is Non Forest Land) located in Village & Mandal Manuguru, District Bhadradri Kothagudem in the state of Telangana. Environmental clearance is not in place.

Est. Value (Rs. Cr)	1473.63
Organisation	Singareni Collieries Company Limited (SCCL)

Contact Details: Bhaskara Rao, Director (Planning & Projects), Po: Kothagudem Collieries, Dist: Bhadradri, Telangana - 507101. Phone: 08744-242602, Fax: 242724, Email: dpp@scclmines.com, gm_env@scclmines.com

Sno. 32	Project Stage: Contract Award
Sector: Consultancy Services	Location: Meghalaya

Project Name / Title	Consultancy projects for Meghalaya roads

Details: Dhruv Consultancy Services has received a letter of acceptance (LoA) for providing consultancy services for a project in Meghalaya. The scope of work includes conducting feasibility study, detailed project report (DPR) prepartion towards Mawngap - Mawphlang- Laitmusiang - Mawkyrwat - Rangthong - Nonghah - Dirang - Khadphra (Ranikor) road section covering 96-km. The contract period will be of nine months.

Est. Value (Rs. Cr)	2.39
Organisation	Dhruv Consultancy Services Limited

Contact Details: Tanvi Tejas Auti, Managing Director, 501, Pujit Plaza, Palm Beach Road, Sector-11, Near CBD Station, Opp K-Star Hotel, CBD Belapur, Navi Mumbai, Maharashtra - 400614 Phone: 09619497305, Email: info@dhruvconsultancy.in

Sno. 33	Project Stage: Tendering
Sector: Crane	Location: *Mumbai* Maharashtra

Project Name / Title	15/5 Ton crane at Bhandup Complex

Details: MCGM plans to assign the supply, installation, testing & commissioning of 15/5 Ton capacity Electrically operated crane at 1910 MLD Pumping Station, Bhandup Complex. Bids are currently invited.

Est. Value (Rs. Cr)	NA
Organisation	Municipal Corporation of Greater Mumbai

Contact Details: P. J. Shinde, Deputy Hydraulic Engineer (Bhandup Complex), 2nd floor, Administrative Building, Khindipada, Mulund West, Mumbai – 400082. Phone: 022-25658514, Mobile: 9167494182, Email: dyhebc@yahoo.com

Sno. 34	Project Stage: Conceptual/Planning
Sector: Defence	Location: NA

Project Name / Title	Helicopter manufacturing unit in India

Details: The Defence Ministry is re-evaluating its plan to manufacture helicopters in India for the navy in collaboration with a foreign partner.

Est. Value (Rs. Cr)	21000
Organisation	Ministry of Defence, Govt of India

Contact Details: Ajay Kumar, Secretary, South Block, New Delhi - 110011. Phone: 011-23012380, Fax: 23010044

Sno. 35	Project Stage: Contract Award
Sector: Defence	Location: NA

Project Name / Title	Supply order from Indian Air Force

Details: Bharat Dynamics Limited has received order towards supply of MRSAM Missile Sections for Indian Air Force deliverables. The order has to be executed in next 24 months.

Est. Value (Rs. Cr)	293.33
Organisation	Bharat Dynamics Limited

Contact Details: 1) Commodore Siddharth Mishra (Retd), Chairman & Managing Director, Plot No. 38-39, TSFC Building, Near ICICI Towers, Financial District, Nanakramguda, Hyderabad-500032. Phone: 040-23456101, 23456145; Fax: 23456110, Website: http://www.bdl-india.in 2) Arup Kumar Maiti, General Manager (Corp. Services), Phone: 040-23007308, 23456160

Sno. 36	Project Stage: Tendering
Sector: Dehumidifiers	Location: Alappuzha district Kerala

Project Name / Title	Supply of Dehumidifiers at Kayamkulam

Details: NTPC Limited invites online bids for the Supply, supervision of erection and commissioning of Dehumidifiers for Preservation of HRSG for NTPC, Kayamkulam.

Est. Value (Rs. Cr)	NA
Organisation	NTPC Limited

Contact Details: 1) T. V. Rao, AGM (C&M), Simhadri Super Thermal Power Station, SSC, Admin Building Annex Via Parawada, PO NTPC – Simhadri, Visakhapatnam, A.P. – 531020. Phone: 08924-284830, Email: tvrao02@ntpc.co.in 2) P Sivakumar, Sr Mgr (Purchase), Mobile: 9573144600, Email: psivakumar@ntpc.co.in

Sno. 37	Project Stage: Conceptual/Planning
Sector: Diesel Engine	Location: *Rajkot* Gujarat

Project Name / Title	Diesel Engines unit at Rajkot

Details: The company has decided to set up Diesel Engines unit at Rajkot Gujarat. The unit will have 3000 Number capacity.

Est. Value (Rs. Cr)	NA
Organisation	Escorts Limited

Contact Details: Nikhil Nanda, Chairman and Managing Director, 15/5, Mathura Road, Faridabad - 121003, Haryana. Phone: 0129-2250222, Fax: 2250023

Sno. 38	Project Stage: Conceptual/Planning
Sector: Drugs / Pharma	Location: *Ankleshwar* Gujarat

Project Name / Title	Capacity expansion of bulk drug unit at Ankleshwar

Details: Cadila Healthcare Limited plans to implement capacity expansion of Bulk Drug & Bulk Drug Intermediates from 64.3 MT/ Month to 199 MT/ Month in existing unit located at Plot No. 291, GIDC Estate, Ankleshwar, Dist. Bharuch, Gujarat - 393002. Environment clearance is sought.

Est. Value (Rs. Cr)	205
Organisation	Cadila Healthcare Limited

Contact Details: 1) Pankaj Patel, Chairman, Zydus Corporate Park, Scheme No.63, Survey No. 536, Khoraj (Gandhinagar), Nr. Vaishnodevi Circle, Sarkhej - Gandhinagar Highway, Ahmedabad - 380015, Gujarat. Phone: 079-26868100, 26868101 - 103, Fax : 26862365 2) Nitin Shah, DGMEHS, Plot No. 291, GIDC Estate, Ankleshwar, Dist. Bharuch, Gujarat - 393002. Phone: 02646-660450, Email: nitin.shah@zyduscadila.com

Sno. 39		Project Stage: Conceptual/Planning
Sector: Drugs / Pharma		Location: Bharuch District Gujarat
Project Name / Title	Bulk Drug & Intermediates Manufacturing Unit at Ankleshwar	
Details: Ozone Life Science plans to set up Bulk Drug & Bulk Drug Intermediates Manufacturing Unit at Plot No. 8006/2, GIDC Industrial Estate, Ankleshwar, Tal - Ankleshwar, Dist - Bharuch, Gujarat. Environmental clearance is sought.		
Est. Value (Rs. Cr)	4.85	
Organisation	Ozone Life Science	
Contact Details: 1) Dilipbhai Z. Patel, Partner, Plot no. 8006/2, GIDC Estate, Ankleshwar, District Bharuch, Gujarat - 393002. Mobile: 9825296260, Email: ozonelifescience@gmail.com 2) Samir Patel, Mobile: 9879190556, 3) Bhavik Patel, Mobile: 9898946447		

Sno. 40		Project Stage: Conceptual/Planning
Sector: Drugs / Pharma		Location: Bharuch District Gujarat
Project Name / Title	Bulk drug mfg unit at Ankleshwar	
Details: Varda Life Science LLP proposes to set up a bulk drug and bulk drug intermediates unit at GIDC Industrial Estate, Ankleshwar. Environmental clearance is sought.		
Est. Value (Rs. Cr)	3	
Organisation	Varda Life Science LLP	
Contact Details: Jigar Patel, Partner, Plot no.3202/A/2, GIDC Industrial Estate, Ankleshwar, Dist-Bharuch, Gujarat-393002 Phone: 0261-2461241, Email: jigarpatel.mba@gmail.com		

Sno. 41		Project Stage: Conceptual/Planning
Sector: Drugs / Pharma		Location: *Vadodara* Gujarat
Project Name / Title	Expansion of bulk drug unit at Vadodara	
Details: Apicore Pharmaceuticals Private Limited plans to undertake the expansion of Bulk Drugs and Bulk Drug Intermediates Manufacturing Unit from 5000 kg/Month to 1697.32 kg/Month at Block No. 252-253, Village: Dhobikuwa, Opposite Jain Irrigation, Padra-Jambusar Road, Taluka: Padra, District- Vadodara. Environment clearance is sought.		
Est. Value (Rs. Cr)	8.88	
Organisation	Apicore Pharmaceuticals Private Limited	
Contact Details: 1) Dr. Ravishanker Kovi, President and CEO, Block no. 252-253, Opp. Jain Irrigation Co, Padra-Jambusar Highway, Tal. Padra,Village Dhobikuva-391440, Dist. Vadodara, Gujarat. Phone: 02662-267166 / 267183 / 267177, Email: ravi@apicore.com 2) Sanjay Bhargav, Vice President Operations, Email: srbhargav61@yahoo.co.in 3) Maulik Sutjar. Phone: 02662-267172, Email: maulik.suthar@apicore.com		

Sno. 42		Project Stage: Conceptual/Planning
Sector: Drugs / Pharma		Location: *Kangra* Himachal Pradesh
Project Name / Title	Cefaclor Oral Suspension unit at Kangra	
Details: Kwality Pharmaceuticals Ltd plans to set up Cefaclor Oral Suspension unit at Kangra, Himachal Pradesh. The unit will have 10000000 Numbers capacity.		
Est. Value (Rs. Cr)	NA	
Organisation	Kwality Pharmaceuticals Limited	
Contact Details: 1) Ramesh Arora, Managing Director, 6th Mile Stone, Majitha Road, Village Nagkalan, Amritsar, Punjab-143601. Phone: 8558820861-62-63-64, Mobile: 9814052314, Email: ramesh@kwalitypharma.com 2) Aditya Arora, Director, Mobile: 9815745569		

Sno. 43	**Project Stage:** Conceptual/Planning
Sector: Drugs / Pharma	**Location:** *Bengaluru* **Karnataka**
Project Name / Title	Human insulin unit at Bengaluru

Details: The company has decided to set up Human Insulin (RDNA Bulk) unit at Bengaluru in the state of Karnataka. The unit will have 2100 Kgs capacity.

Est. Value (Rs. Cr)	NA
Organisation	Biocon Biologics India Limited

Contact Details: 1) Dr. Christiane Hamacher, Chief Executive Officer and Managing Director,, Plot No.29, P1&31P1, Sy.No. 39&43, Semicon Park, Electronic City Post, Bangalore (Urban), Karnataka-560100. Phone: 080-28082808, 40144014, Fax: 28523423, Email: contact.us@biocon.com 2) Ms. Seema Ahuja, Senior Vice President & Global Head - Corporate Communications, Phone: 080-28082808, Email: seema.ahuja@biocon.com, corporate.communications@biocon.com

Sno. 44	**Project Stage:** Conceptual/Planning
Sector: Drugs / Pharma	**Location:** *SAS Nagar* **Punjab**
Project Name / Title	API manufacturing plant at SAS Nagar

Details: Banstag Life Sciences Limited plans to set up Manufacturing unit for Ethyl Acetate Plant with capacity of 25 TPD, Formaldehyde plant with capacity of 50 TPD and API manufacturing plant with capacity of 1.2 TPD At Village- Malakpur,Lalru, Tehsil- Derabassi, SAS Nagar. Environmental Clearance is sought.

Est. Value (Rs. Cr)	7.52
Organisation	Banstag Life Sciences Limited

Contact Details: Sunil Bansal, Director, H.no. 170, Sector 18-A, Chandigarh (U.T.) -160018. Phone: 0172-2543036, Email: sunilbansal0036@gmail.com, banstagmalakpur@gmail.com

Sno. 45	Project Stage: Conceptual/Planning
Sector: Drugs / Pharma	Location: *Udaipur* Rajasthan

Project Name / Title	Expansion of bulk drugs and intermediate unit at Udaipur

Details: US Amino Private Limited is undertaking the expansion of unit for manufacturing of bulk drugs and intermediate located at Khasra No.588, Near Patwarmandal-Basani Kala, Tehsil-Mavali, District: Udaipur (Rajasthan). The company is seeking reconsideration of Environmental Clearance.

Est. Value (Rs. Cr)	0.85
Organisation	US Amino Private Limited

Contact Details: 1) Nitin Kumawat, Director, Khasra No. 588, Village - Ladana, Teh-Mavli, District: Udaipur, Rajasthan - 313205. Email: usaminoco@gmail.com 2) Ankit Kumawat, Mobile: 9351098506, anksa9838@gmail.com

---

Sno. 46	Project Stage: Conceptual/Planning
Sector: Drugs / Pharma	Location: *Suryapet District* Telangana

Project Name / Title	Bulk Drugs and Drug Intermediates unit in Suryapet

Details: SGR Laboratories Private Limited has proposed to establish Bulk Drugs and Drug Intermediates manufacturing Unit at Dondapadu Village in Suryapet district. Environmental Clearance is sought.

Est. Value (Rs. Cr)	12
Organisation	SGR Laboratories Private Limited

Contact Details: Koti Reddy Appide, Managing Director, Plot No:108, SVCIE, IDA, Jeedimetla, Hyderabad - 500055, Telangana. Phone: 040-23070602, Email: sgrlaboratories@gmail.com

Sno. 47		Project Stage: Conceptual/Planning	
Sector: Dyes and Intermediates		Location: *Churu District* **Rajasthan**	
Project Name / Title	Dyes and Intermediates manufacturing project in Churu		
Details: Krishnum Dyes plans to undertake Dyes & Intermediates manufacturing project of 150 MT/Month (Crude) [{Disperse Azo Dyes (All colours) - 100 MT/Month, Coumarine Dyes (All colours)- 25 MT/Month & Methine Dyes (All colours) -25 MT/Month}], at Khasara no 670/521 of Revenue Village - Untwalia , Tehsil & District - Churu. Environmental clearance is awaited.			
Est. Value (Rs. Cr)	20.21		
Organisation	Krishnum Dyes & Intermediate Private Limited		
Contact Details: Mahesh Kumar, Director, Opposite Narbada Bhawan, Churu, Rajasthan - 331001. Phone: 09314961278. Email: maheshprajapat.churu@gmail.com, gssosho1975@gmail.com			

Sno. 48		Project Stage: Conceptual/Planning	
Sector: Education		Location: *North Goa District* **Goa**	
Project Name / Title	IIT Campus at Guleli		
Details: The Centre has recently approved a detailed project report (DPR) towards the construction of an IIT campus at Guleli in Sattari.			
Est. Value (Rs. Cr)	1500		
Organisation	Indian Institute of Technology (IIT) Goa		
Contact Details: 1) B K Mishra, Director, At Goa College of Engineering Campus, Farmagudi, Ponda-403401, Goa. Phone: 0832-2490894, Email: enquiry@iitgoa.ac.in 2) Mustaque Khan, Private Secretary, Phone: 0832-2490896, Email: pstodirector@iitgoa.ac.in			

Sno. 49		Project Stage: Conceptual/Planning
Sector: Electrical / Electronics		Location: *Panchamahal District* **Gujarat**
Project Name / Title	Electrical Insulators unit at Panchamahal	

Details: The company plans to set up manufacturing unit for Electrical Insulators and Insulating Fitting Of Ceramics at Halol in Gujarat. The unit will have 45000 Numbers capacity. ABPCL is a joint venture between Grasim Industries Limited and Maschinenfabrik Reinhausen GmbH of Germany.

Est. Value (Rs. Cr)	NA
Organisation	Aditya Birla Power Composites Limited (ABPCL)

Contact Details: 1) Rohit Pathak, Chief Executive Officer, Survey No.158-159 Village Meghasar, Halol-Kalol-Road, Panchamahal, Gujarat-389330. Email: abpcl@adityabirla.com 2) Sandeep Gurumurthi, Group Head, Communication & Brand, Aditya Birla Management Corporation Private Limited, Phone: 022-66525000, 24995000, Email: sandeep.gurumurthi@adityabirla.com

Sno. 50		Project Stage: Tendering
Sector: Electrical / Electronics		Location: *Kanpur District* **Uttar Pradesh**
Project Name / Title	400 kV post insulators for Panki TPS	

Details: BHEL has invited bids towards the 400 KV post insulators for 400 kV switchyard for UPRVUNL Panki Thermal Power Station Extn. Bids can be submitted by 22nd May, 2020.

Est. Value (Rs. Cr)	NA
Organisation	Bharat Heavy Electricals Limited (BHEL)

Contact Details: Rajeev Kr Roy Manager, BHEL TBG, 5th Floor, Tower-A, Advant Navis Business Park, Sector-142, Noida, UP-201305. Phone: 0120-6748509, Email: rajeevroy@bhel.in, shipra@bhel.in

Sno. 51	**Project Stage:** Under Implementation
Sector: Electrical / Electronics	**Location:** *Murshidabad* **West Bengal**
Project Name / Title	Electrical works for G+6 storey building at Sagardighi

Details: WBPDCL is undertaking the Construction of (G+6) Storeyed Building at Sagardighi Thermal Power Project of WBPDCL, Murshidabad, West Bengal. Bridge & Roof Co. (India) Ltd is the contractor. As of now, tenders are invited for electrical works.

Est. Value (Rs. Cr)	2.71
Organisation	West Bengal Power Development Corporation Limited (WBPDCL)

Contact Details: Soumen Sengupta, DGM (Civil-M&C), Bidyut Unnanyan Bhaban, Plot No. : 3/C, L.A. Block, Salt Lake City, Sector – III, Kolkata -700098. Phone: 033-23393498, Email: s.sengupta@wbpdcl.co.in

---

Sno. 52	**Project Stage:** Conceptual/Planning
Sector: Ethanol	**Location:** *Bharuch* **Gujarat**
Project Name / Title	Ethanol unit at Bharuch

Details: The company has decided to set up Ethanol unit at Bharuch Gujarat. The unit will have 50 Mt capacity.

Est. Value (Rs. Cr)	NA
Organisation	Gujarat Fluorochemicals Limited

Contact Details: 1) Vivek Jain, Managing Director, Sy.No.16/3, 26 & 27, Taluka Ghoghamba, Ranjitnagar, Panchamahal, Gujarat - 389380. Phone: 02678-248153, Fax: 02641-256072

Sno. 53	Project Stage: Conceptual/Planning
Sector: Ethanol	Location: *Belgaum* Karnataka

Project Name / Title	Ethanol unit at Belgaum

Details: The company has decided to set up (Ethanol) Rectified Spirit/Eetra Neutral Alcohol (Undernatured Ethyl Alcohol Strength By Volume Of 80% Or Higher) unit at Belgaum Karnataka. The unit will have 60 Klpd capacity.

Est. Value (Rs. Cr)	NA
Organisation	Askins Biofuels Private Limited

Contact Details: Ashok J. Aski, Director, No.150/6, Vidya Nagar, Gokak Road, Behind K.E.B., Raibag, Harugeri, Belgaum, Karnataka-591220. Email: ashok.aski@gmail.com

---

Sno. 54	Project Stage: Conceptual/Planning
Sector: Explosives	Location: *Nagpur* Maharashtra

Project Name / Title	Expansion of explosive products mfg capacity at Nagpur

Details: Keltech Energies Limited proposes to undertake expansion of existing & addition of new explosive products at Nagpur. Environmental clearance is sought by the company.

Est. Value (Rs. Cr)	63.17
Organisation	Keltech Energies Limited

Contact Details: 1) S L Chowgule, Managing Director, Sungard - ATS, Embassy Icon, No 3, 7th Floor, Infantry Rd, Vasanth Nagar, Bengaluru, Karnataka 560001. Phone: 080-22257900, Email: info@keltechenergies.com 2) S N Sharma, Sr. GM, Nagpur, Maharashtra - 441103. Phone: 0712-2809201, Email: snsharma@keltechenergies.com

Sno. 55	Project Stage: Conceptual/Planning
Sector: Fertilizers	Location: *Kochi* **Kerala**

Project Name / Title	Capacity Enhancement of Complex Fertiliser Production at Ambalamedu

Details: The Fertilizers and Chemicals Travancore (FACT) Ltd plans to undertake the Capacity Enhancement of Complex Fertiliser Production at Ambalamedu, Kochi. Environmental clearance is awaited.

Est. Value (Rs. Cr)	480
Organisation	The Fertilizers and Chemicals Travancore (FACT) Limited

Contact Details: 1) Kishor Rungta, Chairman & Managing Director, Email: cmd@factltd.com 2) Ajith Kumar T P, General Manager (CD), Phone: 0484-2720443, Email: ajith@factltd.com 3) Mohanchandran M, General Manager (Projects), Phone: 0484-2723326. Email: mohanchandran@factltd.com

---

Sno. 56	Project Stage: Conceptual/Planning
Sector: Fertilizers	Location: *Chittorgarh District* **Rajasthan**

Project Name / Title	Greenfield Ammonium Phosphate Fertilizer Complex at Biliya

Details: HZL proposes to set up a Greenfield Ammonium Phosphate Fertilizer Complex with 1.02 MTPA capacity (2 x 0.51 Million TPA) at Village Biliya, Tehsil & District Chittorgarh. Environmental clearance is sought.

Est. Value (Rs. Cr)	2700
Organisation	Hindustan Zinc Limited

Contact Details: 1) Sunil Duggal, CEO & Director, Phone: 0294-6604115, Email: sunil.duggal@vedanta.co.in 2) Subhendu Mishra, Chief Project Officer, Yashad Bhawan, Girwa, Udaipur, Rajasthan-313004. Phone: 0294-6604013, Fax: 2427734, Email: subhendu.mishra@vedanta.co.in

Sno. 57		Project Stage: Conceptual/Planning
Sector: Floor Tiles		Location: *Morbi* Gujarat
Project Name / Title	Ceramic wall tiles at Morbi	
Details:	The company plans to set up manufacturing unit Of Ceramic Wall Tiles, Vitrified Tiles And Floor Tiles unit at Morbi Gujarat. The unit will have 54000 Mtons capacity.	
Est. Value (Rs. Cr)	NA	
Organisation	Vicon Ceramic Private Limited	
Contact Details:	Amarshi Detroja, Director, S.No.154/P2, B/H.Vivanta Ceramic, Bela Rangpar, Morbi, Gujarat-363642. Phone: 8511000218, Email: viconceramic@yahoo.in	

Sno. 58		Project Stage: Conceptual/Planning
Sector: Floor Tiles		Location: *Morbi* Gujarat
Project Name / Title	Tiles unit at Morbi	
Details:	The company has decided to set up Ceramic Wall Tiles unit at Morbi Gujarat. The unit will have 8500 Mts capacity.	
Est. Value (Rs. Cr)	NA	
Organisation	Italico Ceramic	
Contact Details:	1) Manish Patel, Managing Partner, Sr.No.269P3, Morbi Jetpar Road, Rangpar, Morbi, Gujarat-363642. 2) Jaydeep, Mobile: 9979433000/9925182186, Email: italicoceramic9999@gmail.com	

Sno. 59	**Project Stage:** Conceptual/Planning
Sector: Floor Tiles	**Location:** *Morbi* **Gujarat**
Project Name / Title	Vitrified Tiles unit at Morbi
Details: The company has decided to set up a Ceramic Wall, Floor & Vitrified Tiles unit at Morbi, Gujarat. The unit will have 93000 Tonne capacity.	
Est. Value (Rs. Cr)	NA
Organisation	Crevita Granito Private Limited
Contact Details: 1) Paresh Patel, Director, Sr.No.63P1, 63P6, 66/1, 67, 68, 69/1, 69/2 & 69/3, 8-A, National Highway, Metal Road, At.Matel, Wankaner, Morbi, Gujarat-363622. Mobile: 9909296000, crevitagranito@gmail.com 2) Ravi Patel, Mobile: 9099084583, Email: sales@crestona.com,	

Sno. 60	**Project Stage:** Conceptual/Planning
Sector: Forgings	**Location:** *Gurugram* **Haryana**
Project Name / Title	Driveline Aggregates unit at Gurugram
Details: The company has decided to set up Differential Assemblies and Driveline aggregates unit at Gurugram, Haryana. The unit will have 2000000 Numbers capacity.	
Est. Value (Rs. Cr)	NA
Organisation	Sona Blw Precision Forgings Limited
Contact Details: Vivek Vikram Singh, Managing Director, Sona Enclave, Village Begumpur, Khatola, Post Box No. 90, Gurugram, Haryana - 122004. Phone: 0124-4768200, Email: vivek.singh@sonacomstar.com, Website: www.sonagroup.com	

Sno. 61	**Project Stage:** Under Implementation
Sector: Hospitality	**Location:** *Mumbai* **Maharashtra**

Project Name / Title	Four Seasons Private Residences Phase - 1

Details: Provenance Land Private Limited is coming up with Four Seasons Private Residences Phase - 1 at Worli in Mumbai. The built-up area as per approved FSI (In sqmts). Capacite Infraprojects Private Limited is the project contractor. RSP Design Consultants India Private Limited is the Project Architect. Sterling Engineering Consultants Private Limited are the project engineers. The completion date is revised from 31/12/2020 to 31/03/2022.

Est. Value (Rs. Cr)	NA
Organisation	Provenance Land Private Limited

Contact Details: Adarsh Rajkumar Jatia, Managing Director, 1/136, Four Seasons Hotels, Dr. E Moses Road, Worli, Opposite Jijamata Nagar, Maharashtra. Phone: 022-24818910, Website: www.mumbairesidences.com

Sno. 62	**Project Stage:** Under Implementation
Sector: Housing	**Location:** *Mumbai* **Maharashtra**

Project Name / Title	Multi-storey buildings at Girgaum-Kalbadevi

Details: MMRC has recently released its plans for the multi-storey buildings at Girgaum-Kalbadevi. The three towers named Kalbadevi Heights, Kalbadevi Commercial Centre and Girgaon Heights are planned to rehabilitate 734 tenants from the 30 old buildings that were demolished for the Metro-3 (Colaba-Bandra-Seepz). The project will be completed in phases and and ready for occupancy from 2022. The rehabilitation project would also help in widening of the congested JSS Road. As of now, prequalification of contracts is invited towards the construction of high-rises.

Est. Value (Rs. Cr)	395
Organisation	Mumbai Metro Rail Corporation (MMRC)

Contact Details: 1) S.K. Gupta, Director (Projects), Phone: 022-26575102, Email: subodh.gupta@mmrcl.com 2) Anil Kamble, DGM (Civil), MMRCL Transit Office Building, North Side of, City Park Road, E Block, Bandra Kurla Complex, Bandra East, Mumbai - 400051. Phone: 022-26561354, Email: Anil.Kamble@MMRCL.com, Website: www.mmrcl.com

Sno. 63		Project Stage: Tendering
Sector: HVAC		Location: *Raebareli district* **Uttar Pradesh**
Project Name / Title	Air Conditioning work for hospital extension bldg at Unchahar	

Details: NTPC Limited plans to assign the supply, erection, testing and commissioning of Air cooled Package - Air Conditioning work for hospital extension building at NTPC Unchahar Township. Bids are currently invited.

Est. Value (Rs. Cr)	NA
Organisation	NTPC Limited

Contact Details: 1) Neeraj Kumar, AGM (Contracts), SSC NR Auraiya Shared Service Centre, Auraiya Gas Power Station, P O Dibiyapur, District: Auraiya, Uttar Pradesh – 206244, Email: neerajkumar02@ntpc.co.in 2) P K Gupta, Sr Manager (C and M), E-mail: pramodkumargupta@ntpc.co.in

Sno. 64		Project Stage: Under Implementation
Sector: Hydro Power		Location: *West Khasi Hills district* **Meghalaya**
Project Name / Title	Riangdo Small Hydro Power Project	

Details: Riangdo Small Hydro Power Project is coming up at Suanggre Hamegam village in Shahlang under West Khasi Hills district. It is run-of-the-river project. The foundation stone was recently laid.

Est. Value (Rs. Cr)	30
Organisation	Meghalaya Power Generation Corporation Limited (MePGCL)

Contact Details: 1) Smti. A.Nikhla, MCS, Chairman-cum-Managing Director, Lumjingshai, Short Round Road, Shillong-793001, Meghalaya. Phone: 0364-2590610, 2590742 2) M. Shangpliang. Chief Engineer (Gen), Phone: 0364-2591415, Email: cegen.meseb@rediffmail.com

Sno. 65		Project Stage: Tendering
Sector: ICT		Location: *Mandsaur District* **Madhya Pradesh**
Project Name / Title	Centralised monitoring analytical tool for solar plant at Mandsaur	
Details: NTPC has invited tender for Centralised monitoring analytical tool for 250 MW Mandsaur solar PV plant. The completion is targeted in 6 months. Bids are invited upto 18th May, 2020.		
Est. Value (Rs. Cr)	NA	
Organisation	NTPC Limited	
Contact Details: 1) A K Chhabra, Additional General Manager (CM), 6th Floor, EOC, Plot no. A-8A, Sector 24, Noida, Uttar Pradesh - 201301. Phone: 0120-4946680/2410522, Fax: 2410026, Email: akchhabra@ntpc.co.in 2) Harsha, Manager (CM), Phone: 0120-4946628, Email: harsha@ntpc.co.in		

Sno. 66		Project Stage: Conceptual/Planning
Sector: Laminated / Decorative Sheets		Location: *Gandhinagar* **Gujarat**
Project Name / Title	Laminated and Decorative sheets unit at Gandhinagar	
Details: The company has decided to set up High Pressure Laminated Sheets, Decorative Sheets, Plywood And Sun Mica Sheets, Copper Clad unit at Gandhinagar, Gujarat. The unit will have 2000000 Numbers Sheets capacity.		
Est. Value (Rs. Cr)	NA	
Organisation	Ace Mica Private Limited	
Contact Details: Mukesh Kanoi, Director, 12, Agarawal Avenue, 4th Floor, Opp: Navarangpura Telephone Exchange, C.G Rd, Navarangpura, Ahmedabad, Gujarat-380009. Phone: 76228 00001, Email: sales@acemica.com		

Sno. 67	Project Stage: Conceptual/Planning
Sector: Lighting Devices	Location: *Kolkata* West Bengal

Project Name / Title	Supply and installation of Solar studs in New Kolkata

Details: NKDA plans to assign the supply, delivery, installation, commissioning, and testing followed by maintenance for two years of solar road studs of given specifications, to be installed on the parking lane and service lane of Biswa Bangla Sarani, in front of Senior Citizen Park and New Town Mela Ground. The completion period is of two months.

Est. Value (Rs. Cr)	NA
Organisation	New Town Kolkata Development Authority (NKDA)

Contact Details: 1) Animesh Bhattacharya, Chief Executive Officer, 3, Major Arterial Road, Kolkata – 700156. Phone: 033-23242324, Email: ceonkda@gmail.com 2) Sandeep Ganguly, Executive Engineer - I, Phone: 033-23242148, Email: ee1@nkda.in

---

Sno. 68	Project Stage: Tendering
Sector: Material Handling System	Location: *Kokrajhar District* Assam

Project Name / Title	Dry ash handling system for Bongaigaon TPP

Details: NTPC Limited has invited bids towards the Operations and maintenance of Dry ash handling plant of 3x250 MW at NTPC Bongaigaon Thermal Power Project along with related sub systems/auxiliaries on round the clock basis.

Est. Value (Rs. Cr)	4.32
Organisation	NTPC Limited

Contact Details: Nitin Chandra, Sr. Manager(CS) / M K Pattanayak, AGM(CS) / S.S. Sahu, AGM (CS)-I/c, Kaniha, PO-Deepsikha, Distt. Angul, Odisha - 759147. Phone: 06760-247093, 247244, Fax: 243232, Email: nitinchandra@ntpc.co.in / mkpattanayak@ntpc.co.in / sssahu@ntpc.co.in

Sno. 69		Project Stage: Conceptual/Planning
Sector: Metal Alloys		Location: *Valsad* Gujarat
Project Name / Title	Lead Ingots unit at Valsad	
Details: The company has decided to set up Lead Ingots unit at Valsad Gujarat. The unit will have 20400 Mt capacity.		
Est. Value (Rs. Cr)	NA	
Organisation	Genesis Impex (India) Limited	
Contact Details: Rasiklal Rayashi Shah, Managing Director, 101, Awing, Rajshree Tower, Near Pratap Cinema, Kolbad Thane, Maharashtra-400601. Phone: 022-25373061, Email: genesisimpex2007@yahoo.co.in		

Sno. 70		Project Stage: Conceptual/Planning
Sector: Metal Alloys		Location: *Sirmur* Himachal Pradesh
Project Name / Title	M S Ingot unit at Sirmur	
Details: The company has decided to set up M S Ingot unit at Sirmur, Himachal Pradesh. The unit will have 64800 Mt capacity.		
Est. Value (Rs. Cr)	NA	
Organisation	Aditya Industries	
Contact Details: Sanjay Jain, Partner, Nahan Road, Rampur Jattan, Sirmur, Himachal Pradesh-173030. Phone: 01734-325006, Email: adityaeia1@gmail.com		

Sno. 71	**Project Stage:** Contract Award
Sector: Metro Rail	**Location:** *Mumbai* **Maharashtra**
Project Name / Title	Mumbai metro line 7 elevated duct contract

Details: J. Kumar Infraprojects Limited has received Letter of Acceptance from Mumbai Metro Rail Project for construction of Part Design and Construction of balance works of package 1, line 7 elevated viaduct (excluding stations & station viaduct, Architectural finishing & Pre-engineered steel roof structure of station) from chainage Ch (-) 525.903m (Pier P1E) to ch (+) 5801.297m (Pier P 278) Andheri (East)- Dahisar (East) corridor of Mumbai Metro Rail Project of MMRDA.

Est. Value (Rs. Cr)	174.76
Organisation	J. Kumar Infraprojects Limited

Contact Details: 1) Kamal J Gupta, Managing Director, 16-A, Andheri Industrial Estate, Veera Desai Road, Andheri (W), Mumbai-400053. Phone: 022-67743555, Email: info@jkumar.com, website: www.jkumar.com 2) Arvind Gupta, CFO, Phone: 022-67743555, Email: arvind.gupta@jkumar.com

Sno. 72	**Project Stage:** Under Implementation
Sector: Metro Rail	**Location:** *Mumbai* **Maharashtra**
Project Name / Title	Mumbai metro project line 3

Details: MMRC is implementing the 33-km long Aqua Line of the Mumbai Metro, also known as Line 3 or the Colaba–Bandra-SEEPZ line. The corporation has completed tunnelling work on one of the stretches which is 4-km long. The tunnelling work includes construction of five underground stations between CSMT to Mumbai Central through Kalbadevi, Girgaon and Grant Road. The entire tunnelling work of the project will complete by September 2020.

Est. Value (Rs. Cr)	30000
Organisation	Mumbai Metro Rail Corporation (MMRC)

Contact Details: 1) Ranjit Singh Deol, IAS, Managing Director, Transit Office 'E'-Block, North side of City Park, Behind Income Tax Office 'A' Wing Bandra (E) BKC, Mumbai - 400051, Maharashtra. Phone: 022-26575101, Email: ranjitsingh.deol@mmrcl.com 2) Subodh Kumar Gupta, Director (Projects), Phone: 022-26575102, Email: subodh.gupta@mmrcl.com

Sno. 73	**Project Stage:** Under Implementation
Sector: Metro Rail	**Location:** *Mumbai* **Maharashtra**

Project Name / Title	Mumbai metro project line 7
Details: MMRDA is implementing the Mumbai Metro: Dahisar East to Andheri East corridor. The work on the 16.5 km corridor is underway and likely to complete by December 2020.	
Est. Value (Rs. Cr)	4830
Organisation	Mumbai Metropolitan Region Development Authority (MMRDA)
Contact Details: 1) R. A. Rajeev, IAS, Metropolitan Commissioner, MMRDA, Office Building, Bandra-Kurla Complex, Mumbai - 400051. Phone: 022-26594000, Fax: 26591264 2) Dr. Dattatraya Tukaram T, Chief Engineer, Email: chiefengineer1@mailmmrda.maharashtra.gov.in	

Sno. 74	**Project Stage:** Conceptual/Planning
Sector: Oil and Gas	**Location:** *Krishna-Godavari District* **Andhra Pradesh**

Project Name / Title	Expansion of offshore and onshore oil and gas production in KG basin
Details: Cairn Oil and Gas plans to implement take up expansion of Offshore and Onshore Oil and Gas Exploration, Development & Production in existing Ravva Field, PKGM-1 Block (of 331.26 km2) located near Surasniyanam Village (S. Yanam) in Krishna-Godavari, Andhra Pradesh. Environmental Clearance is awaited.	
Est. Value (Rs. Cr)	7924
Organisation	Vedanta Limited (Division Cairn Oil & Gas)
Contact Details: 1) Ajay Kumar Dixit, Chief Executive Officer, DLF Atria, Phase 2, Gurugram – 122002. Phone: 0124-4594454, Email: communications@cairnindia.com 2) Dilip Kumar Bera, Sr. Manager - Environment, 4th Floor, Vipul Plaza, Suncity Sector 54, Gurugram, Haryana - 122002. Phone: 0124-4594176, Email: dilipkumar.bera@cairnindia.com	

Sno. 75	Project Stage: Contract Award
Sector: Oil and Gas	Location: *Golaghat district* **Assam**

Project Name / Title	Numaligarh refinery expansion project

Details: NRL is implementing its refinery expansion project located in Numaligarh in northeastern India. The refining capacity will be expanded from 3 million tonne to 9 million tonne. The project is expected to be completed by 2024. The contract is awarded to thyssenkrupp whose scope of work includes engineering, procurement and construction management (EPCM) services.

Est. Value (Rs. Cr)	300
Organisation	Numaligarh Refinery Limited (NRL)

Contact Details: 1) S K Barua, Managing Director, Phone: Phone: 0361-2203135, 2203129, Email: sk.barua@nrl.co.in 2) Madhuchanda Adhikari, DGM (Corporate Communications), 122A, G.S. Road, Christianbasti, Guwahati-781005, Assam. Phone: 0361-2203140/147, Fax: 2203146, E-mail: madhuchanda@adhikari@nrl.co.in

Sno. 76	Project Stage: Conceptual/Planning
Sector: Oil and Gas	Location: *Tinsukia District* **Assam**

Project Name / Title	Drilling and testing of hydrocarbons in Tinsukia

Details: Oil India Limited plans to undertake the Drilling and Testing of hydrocarbons at 7 locations under Dibru Saikhowa National Park Area, North-West of Baghjan PML in Tinsukia District. Environmental Clearance is sought.

Est. Value (Rs. Cr)	300
Organisation	Oil India Limited

Contact Details: 1) Sushil Chandra Mishra, Chairman & Managing Director, Phone: 0120-2488301, Email: cmd@oilindia.in 2) Pramod Kumar Sharma, Director (Operations), Phone: 0120-2488333 3) Ajaya Kumar Acharya, Head (S&E), Safety & Environment Department, Oil India Limited, Duliajan, Naharkathiya, Dibrugarh, Assam-786602. Phone: 0374-2800542, Fax: 2801796, Email: safety@oilindia.in

Sno. 77		Project Stage: Contract Award
Sector: Oil and Gas		Location: *Begusarai district* **Bihar**
Project Name / Title	\multicolumn{2}{l	}{220/33 kilovolt gas-insulated switchgear (GIS) substation contract from IOCL}
Details:	\multicolumn{2}{l	}{Indian Oil Corporation plans to expand its crude oil processing capacity at its Barauni refinery in Bihar by 50 per cent to 9 million tonne per annum in the next three years. ABB Power Grids has got the 220/33 kilovolt gas-insulated switchgear (GIS) substation contract. ABB will assimilate power from the Bihar State Power Transmission Corporation Ltd and IOCL's captive generation plants and deliver it with efficiency to the Barauni refinery.}
Est. Value (Rs. Cr)	\multicolumn{2}{l	}{165}
Organisation	\multicolumn{2}{l	}{ABB Power Products and Systems India Limited (APPSIL)}
Contact Details:	\multicolumn{2}{l	}{1) Venu Nuguri, Managing Director 2) Manashwi Banerjee, Phone: 080-67143000, 7259766881, Email: manashwi.banerjee@in.abb.com, Poovanna.ammatanda@in.abb.com}

Sno. 78		Project Stage: Conceptual/Planning
Sector: Oil and Gas		Location: *Vadinar* **Gujarat**
Project Name / Title	\multicolumn{2}{l	}{Expansion of refinery at Vadinar}
Details:	\multicolumn{2}{l	}{Nayara Energy Limited plans to undertake the expansion of refinery from 20 MMTPA to 46 MMTPA and Petro-chemical Complex at Vadinar, Dist. Devbhumi Dwarka, Gujarat. Environmental clearance is awaited.}
Est. Value (Rs. Cr)	\multicolumn{2}{l	}{6200}
Organisation	\multicolumn{2}{l	}{Nayara Energy Limited}
Contact Details:	\multicolumn{2}{l	}{1) Asmita Patel, DGM & Head of Environment Section, 4th Floor, Tower 2, Equinox Business Park, Off. Bandra Kurla Complex, LBS Marg, Kurla (West), Mumbai - 400070. Phone: 022-71321010, Fax: 67082177, Email: refinery@nayaraenergy.com 2) Khambhalia, P.O.Box.24, District: Devbhumi Dwarka, Gujarat - 361305. Phone: 02833-661444, Fax: 662929, www.nayaraenergy.com}

Sno. 79		Project Stage: Conceptual/Planning
Sector: Oil and Gas		Location: *Jaisalmer District* **Rajasthan**
Project Name / Title	Expansion of existing 17 production wells in Jaisalmer	
Details: Focus Energy Limited plans to take up expansion of existing 17 production wells and gas production & processing facilities to 522 Gas production/development wells, 5 Gas production and processing facilities each of 65 mmscf/d (including CO2 removal facility) and 40 appraisal wells, located at Block- RJON/6, Village- Langtala, Tehsil & District- Jaisalmer. Environmental clearance is sought.		
Est. Value (Rs. Cr)	2570	
Organisation	Focus Energy Limited	
Contact Details: 1) Avilash Kumar, Head - New Projects, Plot No.6, Sector-32, Gurgaon, Haryana - 122001. Phone: 0124-4385527/28, Email: info@focusenergy.co.in 2) Tara Dutt Bhatt, DGM, 3rd Floor, Gopala Towers, 25 Rajendra Place,,Karol Bagh,Central,Delhi-110008. Phone: 011-25747696, Fax: 25751938, Email: bhatt@focusoil.com.		

Sno. 80		Project Stage: Conceptual/Planning
Sector: Pesticides		Location: *Krishnagiri District* **Tamil Nadu**
Project Name / Title	Pesticide unit at Pochampalli	
Details: Godavari Farm Chemical Industries Private Limited proposes to establish Pesticides - Technical Grade Products Manufacturing Unit at Plot No. 113, SIPCOT's Industrial Complex - Bagur, Parandipalli Village, Pochampalli Taluk, Krishnagiri District, Tamil Nadu. Environmental clearance is awaited.		
Est. Value (Rs. Cr)	9.01	
Organisation	Godavari Farm Chemical Industries Private Limited	
Contact Details: RVR Nagesh, Director, Plot No. 113, SIPCOT's Industrial Complex - Bagur, Parandipalli Village, Pochampalli Taluk, Krishnagiri District, Tamil Nadu-600122. Mobile: 9885560011, Email: godavarifarm19@gmail.com		

Sno. 81		Project Stage: Conceptual/Planning
Sector: Petrochemical		Location: *Vadodara* **Gujarat**
Project Name / Title	Expansiion of petrochemical manufacturing capacity at Vadodara	

Details: Reliance Industries Limited is implementing the expansion and debottlenecking of existing petrochemical manufacturing facility at Vadodara Manufacturing Division. Environmental clearance is sought.

Est. Value (Rs. Cr)	2270
Organisation	Reliance Industries Limited (RIL)

Contact Details: Udayabhaskar Gullapalli, Sr. Vice President Environment, Bldg. No. 7, B Wing, 2nd Floor, Reliance Corporate Park, Thane Belapur Road, Ghansoli, Navi Mumb-400701. Phone: 022-44789038, Email: udayabhaskar.gullapalli@ril.com

Sno. 82		Project Stage: Conceptual/Planning
Sector: Pipes / Pipe Fittings		Location: *Bengaluru (Urban)* **Karnataka**
Project Name / Title	PVC Pipes unit at Bengaluru	

Details: The company has decided to set up Pvc/Cpvc/Swr Pipes and Fitting unit at Bengaluru in the state of Karnataka. The unit will have 50000 Mt capacity.

Est. Value (Rs. Cr)	NA
Organisation	Ashirvad Pipes Private Limited

Contact Details: 1) Pawan Poddar, Managing Director, 4B, Anekal Taluk, Hosur Road, Attibele Industrial Area, Bengaluru, Bangalore(Urban), Karnataka-562107. Phone: 080 28061000, 61342222, Email: pawan.p@ashirvad.com, info@ashirvad.com 2) Sainath G S, Head - Sales Operations, Email: sainath@ashirvad.com

Sno. 83	**Project Stage:** Tendering
Sector: Pipes / Pipe Fittings	**Location:** *Ratnagiri* **Maharashtra**
Project Name / Title	Procurement of MS Pipes for RGPPL
Details: NTPC Limited has invited bids towards the Procurement of PP Lined MS Pipes for handling Acid, Caustic & Chemicals. Bids are invited upto 29th May, 2020.	
Est. Value (Rs. Cr)	NA
Organisation	RGPPL (Ratnagiri Gas and Power Private Limited.)
Contact Details: Gautam Kumar, Manager (C&M), C & M Department, AT & PO: Anjanwel, Taluka: Guhagar, Dist.: Ratnagiri, Maharashtra - 415 634. Phone: 02359-241104, E-mail: gautam.kumar@site.rgppl.com	

Sno. 84	**Project Stage:** Conceptual/Planning
Sector: Plastic Products	**Location:** *Jagatsinghpur* **Odisha**
Project Name / Title	Plastic Containers unit at Paradeep
Details: Glen Industries plans to set up Plastic Food Containers & Moulded paper products manufacturing unit with annual capacity of 9,216 MT at Paradeep Plastic Park, Dist: Jagatsinghpur. SLSWCA in-principle approved the proposal of the company in Feb, 2020.	
Est. Value (Rs. Cr)	63.6
Organisation	Glen Industries Private Limited
Contact Details: Lalita Agrawal, Director, 5OA , Block C, New Alipore, 2nd Floor Raj Veena, Kolkata - 700053. Phone: 033=40019802/03/04 Fax: 24883824, Email: info@glen-india.com, Website: www.glen-india.com	

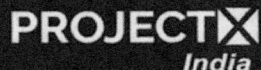

Sno. 85	Project Stage: Conceptual/Planning
Sector: Polymers	Location: *Mehsana District* Gujarat

Project Name / Title	Acrylate polymers unit in Mehsana

Details: Corel Pharma Chem plans to set up synthetic organic chemicals (Acrylate Polymers) unit at Survey No. 473 & 481, Borisana Village, Kadi Thol Road, Kadi, Dist: Mehsana, Gujarat. Environmental Clearance is sought.

Est. Value (Rs. Cr)	20
Organisation	Corel Pharma Chem Private Limited

Contact Details: Kirit Rambhai Patel, Director, Corel House, Opp. Bhagwat Petrol Pump, S. G. Highway, Gota, Ahmedabad – 382 481, Gujarat. Phone: 8000880011 / 22 / 33, Email: kirit@corelpharmachem.com, corel@corelpharmachem.com

---

Sno. 86	Project Stage: Contract Award
Sector: Power	Location: *Ambala* Haryana

Project Name / Title	220 & 66 KV Transmission lines in Yamuna Nagar

Details: Salasar Techno Engineering Limited has secured order for Construction of 220 & 66 KV Transmission lines in Yamuna Nagar & Ambala Area on turnkey basis received from Haryana Vidyut Prasaran Nigam Limited.

Est. Value (Rs. Cr)	28.65
Organisation	Salasar Techno Engineering Limited

Contact Details: Shashank Agarwal, Managing Director, E-20, South Extension - I, New Delhi – 110049. Phone: 8938802180, 7351991000, Fax: 011-45823834, Email: marketing@salasartechno.com

Sno. 87	Project Stage: Commissioned
Sector: Power	Location: *Gurugram* **Haryana**

Project Name / Title	Gurgaon Palwal Transmission Project (GPTL)

Details: Transmission solutions provider has commissioned Gurgaon Palwal Transmission Project (GPTL) in Haryana. The project will evacuate 2,000 MW to Haryana Vidyut Prasaran Nigam through four 400kV double circuit transmission lines with total length of 143 km, three gas Insulated Substations (GIS) at Prithla, Kadarpur and Sohna Road, two bay extensions at Dhanonda and a LILO connecting the 400 kVDC Gurgaon-Manesar transmission line.

Est. Value (Rs. Cr)	1027
Organisation	Sterlite Power Transmission Limited

Contact Details: 1) Anil Agarwal, Chairman 2) Manish Agarwal, CEO - Solutions Business (Products and EPC), Unit 202 Pentagon Tower II, Magarpatta Township, Hadapsar, Pune, Maharashtra - 411028. Phone: 020-66235700, Email: manish.agarwal@sterlite.com, Website: www.sterlitetechnologies.com

Sno. 88	Project Stage: Project Update
Sector: Power	Location: *Angul* **Odisha**

Project Name / Title	Expansion of Talcher TPS

Details: NTPC Limited plans to expand thermal power plant capacity of Talcher Thermal Power Station, located at: Talcher, Dist: Angul. The High Level Clearance Authority (HLCA) of Govt. of Odisha has asked the company to take up CSR activities for the 4 districts of Angul, Dhenkanal, Deogarh and Sambalpur for strengthening of higher education institution (High School, College andTechnical Institutions) at an approx. cost of Rs.500 crore.

Est. Value (Rs. Cr)	NA
Organisation	NTPC Limited

Contact Details: Pratap Sahoo, Sr. Manager (CS) , Talcher Super Thermal Power Station, P.O. : Deepshikha, Angul District, Odisha - 759147. Phone: 06760-247253 Fax: 243232, E-mail: pratapsahoo@ntpc.co.in

Sno. 89	Project Stage: Project Update
Sector: Power	Location: *Jharsuguda District* **Odisha**

Project Name / Title	Thermal power plant at Tareikela

Details: NLC India Limited has proposed to set up 2,400-MW Talabira thermal power project at Tareikela in Jharsuguda District. The High Level Clearance Authority (HLCA) of Govt. of Odisha has asked the company to take up CSR projects worth approx. Rs.500.00 crore for the development of educational infrastructure in the specified districts of Odisha. The Expert Appraisal Committees (EAC) has recently deferred environment clearance for the project, and has asked the company to revise the EIA report.

Est. Value (Rs. Cr)	NA
Organisation	NLC India Limited

Contact Details: 1) Rakesh Kumar, Chairman cum Managing Director, Block - 1, Cuddalore District, Neyveli, Tamil Nadu - 607801. Phone: 04142-252280, Email: cmd@nlcindia.in   2) Prabhakar Chowki, Director (Mines), Phone: 04142-252270, Email: director.mines@nlcindia.in

---

Sno. 90	Project Stage: Tendering
Sector: Pre-engineered Bldg	Location: *Mumbai* **Maharashtra**

Project Name / Title	Three-storey isolation wards at Kasturba Gandhi Hospital

Details: The civic body plans to build a three-storey isolation ward at Kasturba Gandhi Hospital. The pre-engineered building (PEB) technique will be used to construct isolation ward with a capacity of 60 beds. Kinjal Civil Con LLP is the lowest bidder for the project. The contract is yet to be awarded. The completion is targeted in 3 months.

Est. Value (Rs. Cr)	NA
Organisation	Municipal Corporation of Greater Mumbai

Contact Details: Babasaheb Salve, Deputy Chief Engineer (Health infrastructure cell), 3rd floor, Engineering Hub Building, Dr.E.Moses Road, Worli Naka, Worli, Mumbai - 400018. Phone: 022-24958001, Email: dyche01hic.pd@mcgm.gov.in

Sno. 91	Project Stage: Tendering
Sector: Railways	Location: *Tirupati* Andhra Pradesh

Project Name / Title	Redevelopment of Tirupati railway station

Details: RLDA is implementing the redevelopment of Tirupati railway station in the state of Andhra Pradesh. Pre-bid meeting was recently attended by more than 25 infrastructure firms. The contract will be awarded by mid-June 2020.

Est. Value (Rs. Cr)	510
Organisation	Rail Land Development Authority (RLDA)

Contact Details: 1) Ved Parkash Dudeja, Vice Chairman, Unit No. 702-B, 7th Floor Konnectus Tower-II, DMRC Building, Ajmeri Gate, New Delhi-110002. Phone: 011-23233518, Email: cpmrldasc@gmail.com 2) Anjani Kumar, Member/Projects, Mobile: 9717631051, Email: mprojects@rlda.railnet.gov.in

Sno. 92	Project Stage: Contract Award
Sector: Railways	Location: Delhi

Project Name / Title	Regional Rapid Transit System (RRTS) contract

Details: Bombardier Transportation has got an order from National Capital Region Transport Corporation (NCRTC) to supply 210 commuter and metro cars for the Delhi–Meerut Regional Rapid Transit System under Phase 1 of the Regional Rapid Transit System (RRTS).

Est. Value (Rs. Cr)	2577
Organisation	Bombardier Transportation India Private Limited

Contact Details: Rajeev Joisar, Country Leader - India, ERDA Road, Maneja, Vadodara - 390013, Gujarat. Phone: 0265-6198700, Fax: 2638955

Sno. 93	**Project Stage:** Under Implementation
Sector: Railways	**Location:** *Hyderabad* **Telangana**
Project Name / Title	Cherlapally Railway Terminal development

Details: South Central Railways plans to develop the Cherlapally Railway Terminal in an area of 250 acres. So far, only 50 acre of land is available which is sufficient enough to build four more platforms in addition to the current two. The work is going on. Greater Hyderabad Municipal Corporation (GHMC) is constructing the approach road to the terminal.

Est. Value (Rs. Cr)	NA
Organisation	South Central Railway (SCR)

Contact Details: Gajanan Mallya, General Manager, East Maredpally Hyderabad, Telangana. Phone: 040-27822874, Website: http://scrailway.gov.in

---

Sno. 94	**Project Stage:** Conceptual/Planning
Sector: Real Estate	**Location:** *Bengaluru* **Karnataka**
Project Name / Title	Tourist complex at Bengaluru

Details: Nec Real Estate Private Limited has decided to set up Tourist Complex, Commercial Space, Financial Hub, R&D Facilities With Residential Condominium, Service Apartments And Medical City Project unit at Bengaluru.

Est. Value (Rs. Cr)	NA
Organisation	Nec Real Estate Private Limited

Contact Details: Ramesh Yedduri, Director, 8-2-293/82/A/379 & 379A, 2nd Floor, Plot No.379, Road No.10, Jubilee Hills, Hyderabad, Telangana-500033. Phone: 040-23339990, 44557789, Fax: 040-23337789, Email: cs@necltd.com

Sno. 95	Project Stage: Under Implementation
Sector: Real Estate	Location: Mumbai Maharashtra

Project Name / Title	A M Residency project at Mazgaon

Details: Alfa Mana Realtors Pvt Ltd is coming up with A. M. Residency project at Mazgaon in Mumbai. Built-up-area as per Proposed FSI (Proposed but not sanctioned) is 2437.35 sq mts. The project comprises construction of two buildings . The completion date is revised from 30/09/2019 to 29/12/2020.

Est. Value (Rs. Cr)	NA
Organisation	Alfa Mana Realtors Private Limited

Contact Details: Muhammad Saleem Iqbal Motorwala, Director, Shop No. 49, 1st Floor, Kedy Shopping Centre, 233/234 Bellasis Road, Mumbai Central, Maharashtra - 400008. Phone: 022-23010345

Sno. 96	Project Stage: Project Update
Sector: Real Estate	Location: Mumbai Maharashtra

Project Name / Title	Avant Heritage project at Jogeshwari

Details: Aishwarya Avant Builders is coming up with a residential buildings project titled 'Avant Heritage' at Village Majas, Jogeshwari East on 7,605.3 Sq.m. The proposed built-up area is 61,842.89 Sq.m. The project involves construction of 4 buildings with 924 Tenements & 42 Shops. The configuration are as follows: 1) Building 1, Gr+23 Floors, 69.36 Height. 2) Building 2, B+Gr+1 to 3 podium + 4 to 23 Floors, 69.95 Height. 3) Building 3, B+Gr+1 to 3 podium + 4 to 23 floor, 69.60 Height. STP having capacity 490 KLD will be constructed as part of the project. The environment clearance was received on 31st March, 2020.

Est. Value (Rs. Cr)	NA
Organisation	Aishwarya Avant Builders LLP

Contact Details: Manoj Gokulchand Nirmal, Vice President, 522, The Summit Business Bay, Andheri Kurla Road, Off Western Expressway, Near WEH Metro station, Andheri East, Mumbai 400069. Phone: 022-28324155, Email: manoj.nirmal@avantinfra.com

Tracking Projects for your business

Sno. 97	Project Stage: Under Implementation
Sector: Real Estate	Location: *Mumbai* Maharashtra

Project Name / Title	Om Sahil Solitaire Project

Details: Om Sahil Solitaire project is coming up at Sewri, in Mumbai. The Built-up-Area as per approved FSI is 30458.16 sq mt. The project involves construction of five buildings. The completion date is revised from 21/09/2022 to 21/12/2022. As of now, the construction of Building No.1 is completed.

Est. Value (Rs. Cr)	NA
Organisation	Om Sahil Solitaire Builders

Contact Details: Jayant Jaganath Sirsat, Partner, 142, Atlanta Bldg, J.B.Marg, Nariman Point, Mumbai, Maharashtra - 400021. Phone: 022-24922197

Tracking Projects for your business

Sno. 98	Project Stage: Under Implementation
Sector: Real Estate	Location: *Pune District* Maharashtra

Project Name / Title	Green Country Phase-II project

Details: Anand Developers is coming up with a building project titled 'Green Country Phase-II' at S.no.171/7/2, 7/3, 7/4, 7/1, & 171/6K, Pune-Saswad Road, Bhekrai Nagar, Village: Fursungi, Taluka: Haveli, District: Pune. The proposed configuration includes: 1) Wing A with G+11 floors and 34.8 m Height. 2) Wing B with G+P+14 floors and 44.85 Height, and 3) Wing C with G+9 floors and 28.5 Height. The project also involves construction of a Club House with G+1 floor. Total number of tenements: 391. As part of Phase-II, 130 KLD of sewage treatment plant will be constructed. Environment clearance was received in February, 2020.

Est. Value (Rs. Cr)	5.23
Organisation	Anand Developers

Contact Details: Kamlesh Shriniwas Rathod, Partner, Office No. 803, City Square, Shivaji Nagar, Pune, Maharashtra - 411005. Mobile: 9595119000, Email: user@f5realtors.com

Sno. 99	Project Stage: Project Update
Sector: Real Estate	Location: *Thane* **Maharashtra**
Project Name / Title	S K Valley project at Thane

Details: Ittehad Buildcon is coming up with a project titled 'S K Valley' at village Shill, Taluka & District-Thane. The project comprises construction of Residential & Commercial Development on Plot area: 12900.60 Sq mt. The total built-up area would be 37492.67 Sq mt. The project involves construction of 3 buildings with Basement + Ground / Stilt (pt) + 1st to 19th Floor configuration. The Club House/Community Hall with Gr + 1st Floor along with Fitness Centre, and 250 KL Sewage Treatment Plant based on MBBR technology will be built. The environment clearance was received on 31st March, 2020.

Est. Value (Rs. Cr)	130.48
Organisation	**Ittehad Buildcon**

Contact Details: Shabbir Ahmed Khan, Director, Shop No. 1 and 2, S K Residency, Near Toll Naka Bypass, Kausa, Mumbra, Thane, Maharashtra-400612. Phone: 022-65744466, Email: ittehadbuildcon@gmail.com

---

Sno. 100	Project Stage: Contract Award
Sector: Renewable Energy	Location: *New Delhi* **Delhi**
Project Name / Title	400 MW RE power contract award

Details: SECI had invited tenders for the selection of RE Power Developer for Round-the-Clock (RTC) supply of 400 MW RE Power to NDMC, New Delhi, and Dadra & Nagar Haveli under Tariff-based Competitive Bidding (RTC-I). The tender is awarded to ReNew Power at the lowest tariff of Rs 2.9 per kwh (unit).

Est. Value (Rs. Cr)	NA
Organisation	Solar Energy Corporation of India (SECI)

Contact Details: 1) Pratik Prasun, Manager (C&P), D - 3, 1st Floor, Wing - A, Prius Platinum Building, District Centre, Saket, New Delhi - 110017. Phone: 011-71989200, Fax: 71989243, Email : pratikpr@seci.co.in, contracts@seci.co.in 2) Biblesh Meena, Dy. Manager (C&P), Email: 011 71989284

Sno. 101		Project Stage: Under Implementation
Sector: Roads/Highways/Bridges		Location: Arunachal Pradesh
Project Name / Title	Miao to Vijoynagar road project	
Details: The Rural Works Division is implementing Miao to Vijoynagar road project under PMGSY programme. The road works is being divided into five packages. As of March 2020, around 57% of the total length of the road has been completed so far.		
Est. Value (Rs. Cr)	NA	
Organisation	Rural Works Division, Govt of Arunachal Pradesh	
Contact Details: Er. Tatem Bui, Executive Engineer, Rural Works Division, Tezu District Lohit, Arunachal Pradesh. Phone: 03804-223315, Email: eerwdtezu@gmail.com		

Sno. 102		Project Stage: Tendering
Sector: Roads/Highways/Bridges		Location: *Dokmoka* Assam
Project Name / Title	Widening of Dokmoka Loring Thepi Section	
Details: Widening/Improvement to 4 Lane with Paved Shoulder from km 66.000 to km 81.000 (Design Chainage 65.923 to 80.930) of Dokmoka Loring Thepi Section 3 of NH-29 in the state of Assam under Bharatmala Pariyojna on EPC mode. The construction period is of 1.5 years. The bids are invited upto 6th July, 2020.		
Est. Value (Rs. Cr)	165.57	
Organisation	National Highway & Infrastructure Development Corporation Limited (NHIDCL)	
Contact Details: K.C.Bhatt, DGM (Technical), PTI Building, 3rd Floor, 4 Parliament Street, New Delhi-110001. Phone: 011-23461626, Email: kc.bhatt@gov.in		

Sno. 103	Project Stage: Tendering
Sector: Roads/Highways/Bridges	Location: *Loring Thepi* **Assam**

Project Name / Title	Widening of Loring Thepi Ganapath Gaur Gaon Section

Details: Widening/Improvement to 4 Lane with Paved Shoulder from km 81.000 to km 95.400 (Design Chainage 80.930 to 96.400) of Loring Thepi Ganapath Gaur Gaon Section (Package-4) of NH-29 in the state of Assam under Bharatmala Pariyojana on EPC mode. The construction period is of 1.5 years. The bids are invited upto 6th July, 2020.

Est. Value (Rs. Cr)	176.4
Organisation	National Highway & Infrastructure Development Corporation Limited (NHIDCL)

Contact Details: K.C.Bhatt, DGM (Technical), PTI Building, 3rd Floor, 4 Parliament Street, New Delhi-110001. Phone: 011-23461626, Email: kc.bhatt@gov.in

---

Sno. 104	Project Stage: Tendering
Sector: Roads/Highways/Bridges	Location: *Shimla District* **Himachal Pradesh**

Project Name / Title	Balance work of Bridges on Theog Kotkhai Hatkoti section

Details: MoRTH plans to assign the balance work of Bridges on Theog Kotkhai Hatkoti road NH 705 KM 0 to 69 on EPC mode in the state of Himachal Pradesh. The construction period is of 1.5 (Yrs). The bids are invited upto 15th June, 2020.

Est. Value (Rs. Cr)	34.01
Organisation	Ministry of Road Transport & Highways (MoRT&H)

Contact Details: 1) Er.Lalit Bhushan, Engineer-in-Chief (Project), Phone: 0177-2622706, Mobile: 9816128816, Email: hp-sqc@nic.in 2) Er. Archana Thakur, Chief Engineer(NH), Block-D, Nirman Bhawan, HPPWD, Nigam Vihar, Shimla-171002, Himachal Pradesh. Phone/ Fax: 0177-2229416, Mobile: 9418027633, Email: ce-nh-hp@nic.in

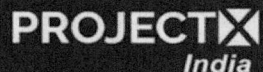

Sno. 105	Project Stage: Tendering
Sector: Roads/Highways/Bridges	Location: *Shimla District* **Himachal Pradesh**

Project Name / Title	Balance work of Bridges on Theog Kotkhai Hatkoti section

Details: MoRTH plans to assign the balance work of Road work culvert protection work and additional road safety work on Theog Kotkhai Hatkoti road on NH 705 from km 00 to 69 in the state of Himachal Pradesh. The construction period is of 1 year. The bids are invited upto 15th June, 2020.

Est. Value (Rs. Cr)	39.91
Organisation	Ministry of Road Transport & Highways (MoRT&H)

Contact Details: 1) Er.Lalit Bhushan, Engineer-in-Chief (Project), Phone: 0177-2622706, Mobile: 9816128816, Email: hp-sqc@nic.in 2) Er. Archana Thakur, Chief Engineer(NH), Block-D, Nirman Bhawan, HPPWD, Nigam Vihar, Shimla-171002, Himachal Pradesh. Phone/ Fax: 0177-2229416, Mobile: 9418027633, Email: ce-nh-hp@nic.in

Sno. 106	Project Stage: Tendering
Sector: Roads/Highways/Bridges	Location: *Bellary District* **Karnataka**

Project Name / Title	Widening of Ibrampura to Tekkalkote road section

Details: MoRTH plans to assign the widening to two lane with paved shoulders from Design Km199.2 (Ex Km.199.300) to Design Km 214.880(Ex Km215.00) of (Ibrampura to Tekkalkote) of NH-150A Jewargi-Chamarajangar section in the State of Karnataka on Engineering, Procurement and Construction basis. The construction period is of 18 months. The bids are invited upto 3rd June, 2020.

Est. Value (Rs. Cr)	93.11
Organisation	Ministry of Road Transport & Highways (MoRT&H)

Contact Details: N Shivakumar, Executive Engineer, National Highway Division, Chitradurga, Karnataka. Phone: 08194-230443, Email: enhcta@gmail.com

Sno. 107		Project Stage: Under Implementation
Sector: Roads/Highways/Bridges		Location: *Mumbai* **Maharashtra**
Project Name / Title	Delhi-Mumbai Expressway project	
Details: Delhi-Mumbai Expressway project covering 1,320-Km-Long is underway. It is touted to be India's longest expressway project. The construction work is being carried out on 18 stretches out of 51. The project is likely to complete by 2022.		
Est. Value (Rs. Cr)	100000	
Organisation	National Highways Authority of India (NHAI)	
Contact Details: Rohin Kumar Gupta, General Manager (T), G-5 & 6, Sector-10, Dwarka, New Delhi-110075. Phone: 011-25074100/200 (Extn: 1111), E-mail: rohingupta@nhai.org		

Sno. 108		Project Stage: Tendering
Sector: Roads/Highways/Bridges		Location: *Barnala District* **Punjab**
Project Name / Title	Widening of Kirshal-Chaura road section	
Details: MoRTH plans to assign the rehabilitation and upgradation from Ch. 164.100 to 182.750, 190.050 to 201.000, 211.075 to 212.475, 221.555 to 224.350 and 225.250 to 227.900 on Barnala Mansa Sardulgarh in the State of Punjab on EPC mode. The construction period is of 1.5 years. The bids are invited upto 29th May, 2020.		
Est. Value (Rs. Cr)	132.27	
Organisation	Ministry of Road Transport & Highways (MoRT&H)	
Contact Details: Er. T S Chahal, Chief Engineer NH, Punjab PWD (B&R Br.), Nirman Bhawan, Block-C, Mini Secretariat, Patiala, Punjab. Phone: 0172-2740197		

Sno. 109	Project Stage: Under Implementation
Sector: Roads/Highways/Bridges	Location: *Jaipur* Rajasthan

Project Name / Title	Sodala elevated road project in Jaipur

Details: The Jaipur Development Authority (JDA) has began construction work on the Sodala elevated road. The elevated road is being constructed from Ambedkar Circle to Sodala. The work is likely to complete by March, 2021 instead of the earlier deadline of November, 2020. Simplex Infrastructures is implementing the project.

Est. Value (Rs. Cr)	250
Organisation	Jaipur Development Authority (JDA)

Contact Details: 1) T. Ravikanth, Commissioner, Main Block - Second Floor -> MB-SF-202, Ram Kishor Vyas Bhawan, Indra Circle, Jawaharlal Nehru Marg, Jaipur-302004 Rajasthan. Phone: 141 2569696 Extn 7202, Fax: 2563035, Email: jdc.jda@rajasthan.gov.in 2) Madan lal Chaudhary, Chief Engineer, Phone:141 2569696 Extn 7306, Fax: 2561785, Mobile: 9829072300

Sno. 110	Project Stage: Under Implementation
Sector: Roads/Highways/Bridges	Location: *Hyderabad* Telangana

Project Name / Title	Construction of link roads connecting highways in Hyderabad

Details: The civic body has undertaken the construction of link roads and slips roads connecting to national highways for the vehicles coming into the city. Some of these projects include construction of Nagole - Bandalguda - Firjadiguda covering 4-km length, Bathukamma Ghat to Boduppal road covering 1.2-km length, and widening of Chengicherla – Cherlapally road.

Est. Value (Rs. Cr)	NA
Organisation	Greater Hyderabad Municipal Corporation (GHMC)

Contact Details: 1) Lokesh Kumar D.S., IAS, Commissioner, RCC Complex Tank Bund Road, Lower Tank Bund, Hyderabad - 500063. Phone: 040-23224564, Email: commissioner-ghmc@gov.in, Website: www.ghmc.gov.in 2) Ziauddin Mohammed, Chief Engineer, Phone: 040-23225397, Fax: 23260050,

Sno. 111	Project Stage: Tendering
Sector: Roads/Highways/Bridges	Location: *Kanpur* Uttar Pradesh

Project Name / Title	Widening of section from Bharthana Chowk to Kodarkoot

Details: MoRTH plans to assign the widening & strengthening of section from Bharthana Chowk to Kodarkoot (Km. 0.00 to Km. 40.00) of NH-91A in the state of Uttar Pradesh on EPC Mode. The construction period is of 18 months. The bids are invited upto 5th June, 2020.

Est. Value (Rs. Cr)	181.84
Organisation	Ministry of Road Transport & Highways (MoRT&H)

Contact Details: 1) S.A.Usmani, Superintending Engineer, NH Circle, PWD, 12/476 Macrobertganj Kanpur-208001, Uttar Pradesh. Email: nhcirclekanpur@gmail.com 2) R R Singh, Chief Engineer(NH), Uttar Pradesh PWD, NirmanBhawan, 96, Mahatma GandhiMarg, Lucknow-226001. Phone: 0522-2236046, Email: cenh.up@gmail.com

Sno. 112	Project Stage: Under Implementation
Sector: Roads/Highways/Bridges	Location: *Noida* Uttar Pradesh

Project Name / Title	Bridge across Hindon river

Details: The Greater Noida Industrial Development Authority (GNIDA) has resumed construction of a bridge between Noida and Greater Noida across the river Hindon River.

Est. Value (Rs. Cr)	65
Organisation	Greater Noida Industrial Development Authority (GNIDA)

Contact Details: 1) Narendra Bhooshan, (IAS), Chief Executive Officer, Phone: 0120-2336004, 2336005, Email: ceo@gnida.in 2) Samakant Srivastava, General Manager (Project), Plot No. 01, Knowledge Park-04, Greater Noida, Gautam Budh Nagar, Uttar Pradesh - 201308. Phone: 0120-2336075, 2336030, 31, Fax: 2336006, Email: gmproject@gnida.in

Sno. 113	**Project Stage:** Tendering
Sector: Roads/Highways/Bridges	**Location:** Uttarakhand

Project Name / Title	Strengthening of road on NH-309
Details: MoRTH plans to assign the strengthening work from km 100.00 to Km. 150.00 and Km. 175.00 to Km. 189.00 and road protection work from Km. 128.00 to Km. 175.00 On NH-121 (New NH-309) in the State Of Uttrakhand under NH(O) on EPC mode. The construction period is of 18 months. The bids are invited upto 4th June, 2020.	
Est. Value (Rs. Cr)	29.15
Organisation	Ministry of Road Transport & Highways (MoRT&H)
Contact Details: 1) P.K. Singh, Chief Engineer (NH), PWD, N.H. Circle, Yamuna Colony, Dehradun, Uttarakhand. Phone/ Fax: 0135-2531868, Mobile: 9717457766 2) Er. Om Prakash, Superintending Engineer, Phone: 0135-2530251, Mobile: 9412019348, Email: senh10@rediffmail.com	

Sno. 114	**Project Stage:** Tendering
Sector: Roads/Highways/Bridges	**Location:** Uttarakhand

Project Name / Title	Widening of Kirshal-Chaura road section
Details: MoRTH plans to assign the widening to two lane with geometric improvement from km 205.00 to km 210.00 (Kirshal-Chaura) of NH-121 in the state of Uttarakhand under Annual Plan 2019-20. The construction period is of 1 year. The bids are invited upto 1st June, 2020.	
Est. Value (Rs. Cr)	8.82
Organisation	Ministry of Road Transport & Highways (MoRT&H)
Contact Details: 1) P.K. Singh, Chief Engineer (NH), PWD, N.H. Circle, Yamuna Colony, Dehradun, Uttarakhand. Phone/ Fax: 0135-2531868, Mobile: 9717457766 2) Er. Om Prakash, Superintending Engineer, Phone: 0135-2530251, Mobile: 9412019348, Email: senh10@rediffmail.com	

Sno. 115	Project Stage: Under Implementation
Sector: Roads/Highways/Bridges	Location: *Kolkata* West Bengal

Project Name / Title	Majerhat bridge project

Details: West Bengal Public Works department is implementing the Majerhat bridge reconstruction project. The work had stopped due to the lockdown and has now partially resumed. The completion was targeted by July 2020 which needs to be revised considering the prevailing situation.

Est. Value (Rs. Cr)	400
Organisation	Public Works Department, Govt of West Bengal

Contact Details: 1) Tapas Mukherjee, Engineer-in-Chief & Ex-Officio Secretary, PWD, Writers' Buildings, Kolkata, West Bengal. Phone: Email: eincpwd@wb.gov.in 2) Susmit Banerjee, Chief Engineer (Head Quarter), P W (Roads) Dte.   Nabanna, 8th floor, 325, Sarat Chatterjee Road, Shibpur, Howrah - 711102. Phone: 033-22145959, Fax: 22535225, Email: cepwdroads@gmail.com

Sno. 116	Project Stage: Under Implementation
Sector: Solar Energy	Location: *Gurugram* Haryana

Project Name / Title	100 MW solar projects across the country

Details: Gurugram-based independent power producer JBM Solar plans to setup 100 MW projects by next year. Majority of these projects would be ground-mounted.

Est. Value (Rs. Cr)	NA
Organisation	JBM Solar

Contact Details: Nishant Arya, Executive Director, Plot No.9, Institutional Area, Sector 44, Gurgaon, HR-122003. Phone: 0124-4674500, corp.communications@jbmgroup.com

Sno. 117	Project Stage: Conceptual/Planning
Sector: Solar Energy	Location: *Belgaum* Karnataka

Project Name / Title	Solar power unit at Belgaum

Details: The company has decided to set up Solar Power Plant unit at Belgaum in the state of Karnataka. The unit will have 20 MW capacity.

Est. Value (Rs. Cr)	NA
Organisation	Izra Solar Energy Private Limited

Contact Details: Neeraj Gupta, Director, 138, Ansal Chambers Ii Bhikaji Cama Place, South Delhi, Delhi-110066. Phone: 011- 46772200, Fax: 41112980, Email: honey@renewpower.in

Sno. 118	Project Stage: Tendering
Sector: Solar Energy	Location: *Belgavi* Karnataka

Project Name / Title	360 KWP Solar System at VTU Belagavi

Details: BHEL plans to assign the Supply, Installation & Commissioning of 360 KWP Solar System at VTU, Belagavi. Bids were invited recently in this regard.

Est. Value (Rs. Cr)	0.77
Organisation	Bharat Heavy Electricals Limited (BHEL)

Contact Details: Rajnish Kumar, Dy Manager, BHEL Rudrapur Kichha Bypass Road, Rudrapur, US Nagar, Uttarakhand - 263153. Phone: 05944-257220, Email: rajnishk@bhel.in

Sno. 119	Project Stage: Tendering
Sector: Solar Energy	Location: *Bengaluru* **Karnataka**

Project Name / Title	Type testing of solar PV modules

Details: BHEL has recently invited bids towards the type testing of solar photovoltaic (PV) modules as per IEC & IS standards. Bids are invited upto 30th May, 2020.

Est. Value (Rs. Cr)	NA
Organisation	Bharat Heavy Electricals Limited (BHEL)

Contact Details: Raj Kumar Pradhan, Electric & Photovoltaic Division (EPD), Prof. CNR Rao Circle, Science Institute Post, Malleswaram, Bengaluru - 560012. Phone: 080-22182364, Email: pradhan@bhel.in

Sno. 120	Project Stage: Conceptual/Planning
Sector: Solar Energy	Location: *Kolkata* **West Bengal**

Project Name / Title	1 MW canal top solar project at Bagjola

Details: NKDA plans to install a 1 MW (2X500 kW) canal top solar project at Bagjola Canal located in New Town. The completion is targeted in 12 months.

Est. Value (Rs. Cr)	NA
Organisation	New Town Kolkata Development Authority (NKDA)

Contact Details: 1) Animesh Bhattacharya, Chief Executive Officer, 3, Major Arterial Road, Kolkata – 700156. Phone: 033-23242324, Email: ceonkda@gmail.com 2) Sandeep Ganguly, Executive Engineer - I, Phone: 033-23242148, Email: ee1@nkda.in

Sno. 121	Project Stage: Conceptual/Planning
Sector: Solar Energy	Location: *Murshidabad* **West Bengal**

Project Name / Title	10 MW of grid-connected floating solar project at Sagardighi

Details: WBPDCL plans to set up 10 MW of grid-connected floating solar project at the Sagardighi Thermal Power Project in Murshidabad.

Est. Value (Rs. Cr)	NA
Organisation	West Bengal Power Development Corporation Limited (WBPDCL)

Contact Details: Soumen Sengupta, DGM (Civil-M&C) , Bidyut Unnanyan Bhaban, Plot No. : 3/C, L.A. Block, Salt Lake City, Sector – III, Kolkata -700098. Phone: 033-23393498, Email: s.sengupta@wbpdcl.co.in

---

Sno. 122	Project Stage: Conceptual/Planning
Sector: Sugar	Location: *Satara* **Maharashtra**

Project Name / Title	Sugar factory in Kopergaon

Details: Shivneri Sugars Limited plans to establish 10,000 TCD Sugar Factory (scrapping of existing 800 TCD plant), 60 MW Co-gen Plant (50 MW from Co-gen plant & 10 MW from distillery) and 200 KLPD molasses based distillery at Ganesh Tekadi, Nabhi (Bk.), Kopergaon, Satara. Environmental Clearance is sought.

Est. Value (Rs. Cr)	520
Organisation	Shivneri Sugars Limited

Contact Details: Sushant, Executive Director, A/p. Ganesh tekadi, Nhavi (Bk.), Tal. Koregaon, Dist. Satara, Maharashtra - 416416. Phone: 0233-2373885, Email: sushant.shivneri@gmail.com

Sno. 123	**Project Stage:** Conceptual/Planning
Sector: Sugar	**Location:** *Solapur District* **Maharashtra**
Project Name / Title	Expansion of sugar factory at Watwate

Details: Jakraya Sugar Ltd has proposed expansion of Sugar Factory from 4900 TCD to 7500 TCD (increase by 2600 TCD), Co-generation Plant from 11MW to 30 MW and Molasses/Sugarcane juice based Distillery from 30 KLPD to 200 KLPD at Watwate, Mohol, District Solapur. Environmental clearance is not in place.

Est. Value (Rs. Cr)	141
Organisation	Jakraya Sugar Limited

Contact Details: Sachin Jadhav, Managing Director, A/P - Watwate, Tal. Mohol, Dist. Solapur, Mohol, Solapur, Maharashtra - 413253. Phone: 02188-221173, Email: jakrayadistillery2018@gmail.com, jakrayamd@gmail.com

---

Sno. 124	**Project Stage:** Conceptual/Planning
Sector: Sugar Alcohol	**Location:** *Dhar* **Madhya Pradesh**
Project Name / Title	Sorbitol Solution unit at Dhar

Details: The company has decided to manufacture Sorbitol Solution unit at Dhar Madhya Pradesh. The unit will have 130000 Tons capacity.

Est. Value (Rs. Cr)	NA
Organisation	Kasyap Sweetners Limited

Contact Details: Siddharth Kashyap, Managing Director, 10 Marthanda, 4th Floor, 84 Dr Ab Road, Worli Naka, Worli, Mumbai, Maharashtra-400018. Phone: 022-49194100, Fax: 49194110

Sno. 125	Project Stage: Conceptual/Planning
Sector: Technical Textiles	Location: *Valsad* Gujarat

Project Name / Title	Technical Textile unit at Valsad

Details: The company has decided to set up Technical Textile unit at Valsad Gujarat. The unit will have 5500 Mt capacity.

Est. Value (Rs. Cr)	NA
Organisation	Strata Geosystems (India) Private Limited

Contact Details: Narendra Dalmia, Director, Shabnam House, Ground Flo- Or, Plot No.A 15/16, Central Cross Road B, M.I.D.C. Andheri (E), Mumbai, Maharashtra-400093. Phone: 022-40635100, Fax: 40635199, Email: info@strataindia.com

---

Sno. 126	Project Stage: Under Implementation
Sector: Tourism	Location: West Bengal

Project Name / Title	Bhorer Alo tourism works

Details: The department of tourism is currently undertaking the infrastructure development work at Bhorer Alo, one of the largest tourism project taken up by the state government at Gazoldoba near the Teesta Barrage. The projects comprises construction of a road overbridge over the Teesta canal which is located near the tourism hub in Gajoldoba, a pump house on the site. Apart from this a road will be constructed that will connect Bhorer Alo with the Bengal Safari Park and move through Baikunthapur forest.

Est. Value (Rs. Cr)	NA
Organisation	Department of Tourism, Govt of West Bengal

Contact Details: Kaushik Bhattacharya, I.A.S, Managing Director, New Secretariat Building 1, 3rd Floor, K. S. Roy Road, Kolkata, West Bengal - 700001. Phone: 033-22436440, 23585189,

Sno. 127	**Project Stage:** Tendering
Sector: Transport	**Location:** *Madurai District* **Tamil Nadu**

Project Name / Title	New Bus Stand in Tirumangalam

Details: Tirumangalam Municipality plans to assign the construction of New Bus Stand in Tirumangalam Municipality on Design, Build, Finance, Operate and Transfer (Dbfot) basis. Bids are invited upto 12th June, 2020.

Est. Value (Rs. Cr)	21.72
Organisation	Tirumangalam Municipality

Contact Details: Jeyarama Raja, Municipal Commissioner, Tirumangalam - 625706, Tamil Nadu. Phone: 04549-280757, commr.tirumangalam@tn.gov.in

---

Sno. 128	**Project Stage:** Conceptual/Planning
Sector: Urban Development	**Location:** *Mohali* **Punjab**

Project Name / Title	GMADA to take up internal works in Mohali

Details: GMADA plans to take up internal development works in Mohali's Sectors 100 and 104, comprising the Pearl City project. Based on the Supreme Court directives, the development authority has prepared estimates of Rs.105 crore in this regard.

Est. Value (Rs. Cr)	105
Organisation	Greater Mohali Area Development Authority (GMADA)

Contact Details: 1) Sunil Kansal, Chief Engineer, Room No. 318, PUDA Bhawan, S.A.S Nagar, Punjab - 160062. Phone: 0172-5063022, ce@gmada.gov.in 2) Davinder Singh, Superintending Engineer, Phone: 0172-5063220, sec1@gmada.gov.in

Sno. 129	Project Stage: Tendering
Sector: Waste Management	Location: *Imphal* Manipur

Project Name / Title	Zero Waste Management Plant at Imphal

Details: AAI has invited Job Contract for Zero Waste Management Plant at Imphal International Airport during 2020-21 & 2021-22.

Est. Value (Rs. Cr)	0.21
Organisation	Airports Authority of India

Contact Details: 1) S.K. Panigrahi, Imphal Tulihal-795140, Manipuur. Phone: 0385-2455069, Fax: 2455076. Email :apdimphal@aai.aero, www.aai.aero 2) Assistant General Manager Engg (E)-II, Imphal International Airport, Imphal, Manipur-795140. Mobile: 9560282450, Email: sanjeevkumar@aai.aero, snita@aai.aero

Sno. 130	Project Stage: Tendering
Sector: Water Treatment	Location: *Ranchi* Jharkhand

Project Name / Title	9.5 MLD water treatment plant in Jharkhand

Details: Construction and 5 years of Operation and Maintenance of Water Supply System in Hussainabad (Intake works, Rising main, 9.5 MLD Water treatment plant, Clear water main, Overhead reservoirs, Distribution network and House service connections)

Est. Value (Rs. Cr)	37.44
Organisation	Jharkhand Urban Infrastructure Development Company Limited (JUIDCO)

Contact Details: Ramesh Kumar, Project Director (Technical), 3rd Floor Pragati Sadan Kutchery Road Ranchi 834001.Phone/Fax: 0651-2243203, Mobile: 9431101019, Email: pdt.juidco@gmail.com, juidcolimited@gmail.com.

Sno. 131	Project Stage: Tendering
Sector: Water Treatment	Location: *Surat* Maharashtra

Project Name / Title	O&M of water treatment plant of NTPC Mouda plant

Details: NTPC Limited has invited bids towards assigning the mega contract for operation of water treatment plant stage-I (2x500 MW) and stage-II (2x600 MW) of NTPC Mouda. Bids are invited upto 27th May, 2020.

Est. Value (Rs. Cr)	NA
Organisation	NTPC Limited

Contact Details: 1) Sunny Agarwal, Deputy Manager (Contracts & Materials), Western Region -I Shared Service Centre-Kawas, Simulator Building, Kawas Gas Power Project, PO: Adityanagar Surat- 394516. Phone: 0261-2877988, 2877987, 2860165, Email: sunnyagarwal@ntpc.co.in, bnarasimha@ntpc.co.in, subodhshankar@ntpc.co.in

Sno. 132	Project Stage: Tendering
Sector: Water Treatment	Location: *Gurdaspur* Punjab

Project Name / Title	14 MLD Water Treatment plant in Gurdaspur

Details: Department of Water Supply & Sanitation, Govt of Punjab plans to assign the contract to Design and build all components of the Drinking Water Supply System including 14 MLD capacity Water Treatment Plant along with other works and machinery, for providing bulk supply of water to various villages of Block Dhariwal, Kalanaur, Gurdaspur and Dera Baba Nanak, District: Gurdaspur on DBOT basis. (Number of villages: 102). Bids are currently invited.

Est. Value (Rs. Cr)	76.46
Organisation	Department of Water Supply & Sanitation, Govt of Punjab

Contact Details: Er. Jatinder Singh Saini, Superintending Engineer, Water Supply & Sanitation Circle, Gurdaspur, Village Babri, Amritsar to Pathankot Highway, Gurdaspur, Punjab. Phone: 01874-245217, Email: sewss.gurdaspurpb@yahoo.com

Sno. 133	Project Stage: Tendering
Sector: Water Treatment	Location: *Kanpur* Uttar Pradesh

Project Name / Title	Submersible system for Benajhber WTP

Details: Kanpur Nagar Nigam plans to assign the design, construction and supply of 1 no. submersible system for settling tank at Benajhber Water Treatment plant in Kanpur. Bids are currently invited.

Est. Value (Rs. Cr)	NA
Organisation	Department of Water Supply, Kanpur Nagar Nigam

Contact Details: 1) Akshay Tripathi, Commissioner, Motijheel, Kanpur, Uttar Pradesh. Phone: 2541258, 2531215, Mobile: 8601811111, Email: mckanpur@yahoo.com, kanpur_nagar.nigam@yahoo.co.in 2) Kailash Singh, Chief Engineer (Civil), Mobile: 8601800801

Sno. 134	Project Stage: Conceptual/Planning
Sector: Wax	Location: *Sonipat* Haryana

Project Name / Title	Laminating Wax unit at Sonipat

Details: The company has decided to set up Artificial Wax And Prepared Wax, Laminating Wax unit at Sonipat, Haryana. The unit will have 1000 Tonnes capacity.

Est. Value (Rs. Cr)	NA
Organisation	Chemline India Limited

Contact Details: Dr. Ravindra Goel, CMD, F 1, Sarda Chamber 1, Central Market, Prashant Vihar, Delhi-110085. Phone: 011-27555991 to 99 Email: sales@chemlineglobal.com, ram@chemlineglobal.com

Sno. 135	Project Stage: Conceptual/Planning
Sector: Wind Energy	Location: *Kutch* Gujarat

Project Name / Title	300 MW Wind Energy unit at Kutch

Details: The company has decided to set up Wind Energy unit at Kutch Gujarat. The unit will have 300 Mw capacity.

Est. Value (Rs. Cr)	NA
Organisation	Adani Green Energy Five Limited

Contact Details: Pragnesh Darji, Company Secretary, Adani House, Nr Mithakhali Six Roads, Navrangpura, Ahmedabad, Gujarat - 380009. Phone: 079-25555555, Email: pragnesh.darji@adani.com 2) Udayan Sharma, Deputy General Manager

Sno. 136	Project Stage: Conceptual/Planning
Sector: Wind Energy	Location: *Kutch* Gujarat

Project Name / Title	Wind Energy unit at Kutch

Details: The company has decided to set up Wind Energy unit at Kutch Gujarat. The unit will have 300 Mw capacity.

Est. Value (Rs. Cr)	NA
Organisation	Adani Green Energy Three Limited

Contact Details: Pragnesh Darji, Company Secretary, Adani House, Nr Mithakhali Six Roads, Navrangpura, Ahmedabad, Gujarat - 380009. Phone: 079-25555555, Email: pragnesh.darji@adani.com 2) Udayan Sharma, Deputy General Manager

Tracking Projects for your business

Sno. 137		Project Stage: Conceptual/Planning
Sector: Wires and Cables		Location: *Jhajjar* Haryana
Project Name / Title	S S wire unit at Jhajjar	
Details: The company has decided to set up S S Wire/M S Wire/G I Wire/H B Wire/Articles Of Iron Or Steel unit at Jhajjar Haryana. The unit will have 58000 Mt capacity.		
Est. Value (Rs. Cr)	NA	
Organisation	Garg Inox Limited	
Contact Details: 1) Rahul Verma, Vice President (Marketing), Unit-2, Asaudha Siwan, 43, Milestone, Delhi Rohtak Road, Asoudha, Bahadurgarh - 124507, Haryana. Phone: 01276-222222, Fax: 01276-222000, Email: gargwire@gargwire.com, rmehra80@gmail.com 2) Pranav Bansal, Director		

You can share your project, contract, tender details to feature in ProjectX India.

Email the details to

Editor@ProjectXIndia.com